JESUS, YOUR
Baby
AND YOU

A Guide to Trusting God During Your Pregnancy

HELEN & OLLY
Goldenberg

Printed in the United Kingdom
First published 2015
ISBN 978-0-9928184-2-5

Published by Children Can
  BM Children Can
  London, WC1N 3XX
  United Kingdom

www.childrencan.co.uk
info@childrencan.co.uk

Dedication

To my four amazing sons and my wonderful daughter, who have brought your daddy and I such joy. Seeing God fulfil your destiny one day at a time is a thrill. I love you all with all of my heart!

To Abundant Joy who has helped in the writing of this book. You have fulfilled your destiny in your short life, by contributing immeasurably to this work through the short experience of knowing you as mine. I know I will meet you again one day in heaven.

Contents

Acknowledgements

There are many people who have helped the material in this book become a reality. Thanks to all those who willingly shared their stories in this book. We are so grateful for your openness concerning a very personal part of your life. Without you this book would be so much poorer.

Thanks to Anna Hawken, Gemma Hunt, Pauline Jacob, Lindsay Melluish, Lisa Mayers, Liz Sheridan and Sara Watson. Your encouraging words and insightful feedback based on your expertise and personal experiences has improved this book and saved us from some blunders. Any errors that remain are, of course, our own.

Thanks to Tim Pettingale for your amazing editing skills and great heart. Thanks to Alistair Sanders and family for your friendship and all your work in typesetting and design, and thanks to Stephan Proudfoot for the cover design. Thanks to Jonathan Bugden and the team at Joining the Dots Distribution for their continual support.

Special thanks to Ayo Oyewole and the team in the womb ministry who pioneered this ministry in the early years and for the wonderful declarations at the end of this book.

Finally, we give thanks to God, the creator and giver of life in all its fullness for His continual mercies to us.

Jesus, Your Baby and You

Endorsements

"An inspirational and encouraging book, a must-read for all pregnant women and their husbands! Olly and Helen provide some creative ways to prepare, spiritually, for the momentous change the arrival of a new baby brings. They urge us to discover God's unique destiny for our baby and to pray that that child will become all that God intended."

Lindsay Melluish *Pastor, Speaker, Author, Family Therapist*

✳

"Finally someone wrote the book we've all been wanting! Helen Goldenberg empowers families to see their babies as the powerful kingdom shapers that they are and will be, and equips parents to begin spiritual parenting at the very start of their children's lives in utero. Encouraging, hopeful, and insightful—I would recommend this for all pregnant women and partners!"

Rachel Turner *Family Life Pastor, St Paul's Hammersmith*

✳

"This is a thoughtful, honest & inspiring book for those hoping to have a family or who are already on the journey of pregnancy. The thought-provoking gospel truths about life and God's divine plan are heartwarming and hope filled, reassuring even the most anxious of minds."

Gemma Hunt *Television Presenter*

✳

"Helen and Olly Goldenberg are two of my heroes in the faith. I have partnered with them in ministry and life, seen their struggles and watched God prove Himself strong on their behalf. They are seasoned, proved and fruitful in marriage, family and ministry. You will be blessed by their faith for miracles and in the power of God. This book is full of wisdom from the Holy Spirit, through God's word and through REAL life experiences."

Cathie Clancy *Co-Founder of Overflow Kids, Australia*

"What an encouraging read! This book was really significant in grounding me spiritually and emotionally during my pregnancy and as I thought ahead to labour. Helen and Olly's years of experience shine through and the book is honest, realistic and practical as well as faith-filled and uplifting. For me, it was a beautiful, God-inspired antidote to the barrage of birth horror stories and conflicting advice that others were offering. I will be sharing it with all my pregnant friends."

Anna Hawken *Childrens Pastor, St Pauls church in St Albans*

✳

"This book is as cool water to a parched land. A much, much needed call to Christian men and women to place God at the centre of pregnancy, birth and parenting. This is a fantastic resource with very practical, enjoyable and 'doable' suggestions for thorough spiritual preparation for labour, birth and parenting which can often be overlooked. Helen's inclusive approach makes this book suitable for all types of pregnancy and plans for birth. Her warmth, passion and personal experience as mum of five shines through."

Liz Sheridan *BellyTots Leader and NCT Antenatal Teacher.*

✳

"Along with many other emotions, much of pregnancy can feel mysterious—an unknowable, untouchable miracle that unfolds without much parental intervention or participation until birth. This book warmly invites parents to fully take hold of the spiritual authority God has given them as his partners in the creation of new life. Helen and Olly demonstrate what it means to intentionally sow into your unborn child's shalom, laying foundations of peace, joy and security into their whole being. Their passionate belief in the God-given identity and spiritual capacity of children, even the unborn, leaks out of every page, as it does from their lives and ministry. You will find stories here to inspire faith and trust in the great Designer of your child, your pregnancy and birth. Every word of this book has authenticity, as Helen and Olly have lived what they write, continuing to dynamically and faithfully shepherd their amazing children in God's ways as they grow."

Catherine Kennedy *National Leader for Kings Kids International, YWAM England*

Some words

Preg·nant (adjective)[1]

1. Having a child or other offspring developing in the body; with child or young, as a woman or female mammal.
2. Fraught, filled, or abounding (usually followed by *with*): a silence pregnant with suspense.
3. Teeming or fertile; rich (often followed by *in*): a mind pregnant in ideas.
4. Full of meaning; highly significant: a pregnant utterance.
5. Of great importance or potential; momentous: a pregnant moment in the history of the world
6. Inventive or imaginative
7. Prolific or fruitful

Par·ent (noun)[2]

1. One who begets, gives birth to, or nurtures and raises a child; a father or mother.
2. An ancestor; a progenitor.
3. An organism that produces or generates offspring.
4. A guardian; a protector.
5. A parent company.

v. par·ent·ed, par·ent·ing, par·ents

1. To act as a parent; to raise and nurture.
2. To cause to come into existence; originate.

---

[1] www.dictionary.com

[2] www.thefreedictionary.com

11

Jesus, Your Baby and You

Introduction

*"Yet you brought me safely from my mother's womb
and led me to trust you at my mother's breast. I was
thrust into your arms at my birth. You have been my
God from the moment I was born."*

Psalm 22:9–10

As I start this book, I am now the mother of five gorgeous children. Before I became one, the thought of being a mother was both daunting and amazing.

It doesn't seem that long ago that I was a little girl, copying my mum around the family home. This was followed by teenage and college years, finding out who I was and what I wanted to do with my life, and serving God as a young adult. I had thought about marriage and children, but had not really processed what it would be like to have another human being call me "Mummy"—or even what it would be like to be pregnant.

When I was pregnant with my first child I felt a jumble of emotions with an intensity I'd never experienced before; excitement, joy and fear, all mixed together. I realised that if I was going to make the most of my pregnancy, and not just survive the next nine months, then this journey had to be taken hand in hand with God.

When you first tell people you are pregnant it seems as though everyone has some advice to share with you: "Make sure you get plenty of rest… make sure you stay active…" and much more. I began to feel as others were trying to superimpose their ideals on me, as to how my pregnancy should be—even though my body was telling me something different.

Those who have trod this mysterious path before all have their own story to share with you: "Oh, when I was pregnant…" they begin, before launching into a detailed account of all their traumas and joys. As for the stories about labour, people especially relished sharing those details! Unfortunately for me, however, hearing all these stories built up a negative, fearful picture of how my labour and pregnancy might pan out.

Eventually, being quite a stubborn woman, I'd had enough of it all. "That's it! I want God's best pregnancy and labour," I said. My prayer is that you too will walk through your pregnancy actively seeking God's best for you, for the labour, for your child and your whole family.

Part 1

Ministering to your unborn child

Jesus, Your Baby and You

1

The Unborn Child

God the Creator

What a wonderful, miraculous God we serve. The miracle of conception and the growth of a child within their mother's womb is something to be wondered at. A tiny sperm and egg meet and fuse together, and that egg grows into a full sized baby in 9 months. God knows what He is doing. No one else can take the credit for what God creates within us.

Babies in the womb feel, hear and are aware of their mother and father's voice. As we will see, they are also aware of God whilst in the womb. Your baby can encounter God in the womb in a way that will shape their future lives and help prepare them for their future destiny.

The blessing of children

> "Children are a gift from the Lord; they are a reward from Him. Children born to a young man are like arrows in a warrior's hands. How joyful is the man whose quiver is full of them! He will not be put to shame when he confronts his accusers at the city gates."
>
> Psalm 127:3–5

No matter how you felt when you found out you were pregnant, the children God gives us are a reward. Whether you were excited, panicked or anxious, every child is a blessing. Each child is given by God and is precious to Him. The reward of having a child is immense and the blessing of becoming a family is great.

Children are part of the heritage that God gives to us. Psalm 128 describes them as being, *"like vigorous young olive trees as they sit around your table."* It is a picture of fruitfulness. God gives us children to bless us.

Psalm 127 tells us that our children are *"like arrows in a warrior's hands."* Any believer who has children is appointed by God to be a warrior. It is our duty to engage in battle on behalf of our children. Notice where these arrows are placed in this scripture: in the *hand* of the warrior. Most warriors do not keep arrows in their hands; instead they store them in their quiver. When a warrior takes up an arrow in his hand it's because he is about to use it. Having set the arrow in the bow, it is then aimed, specifically and directly, at its target. The arrows have a purpose and a destiny.

In other words, if we are going to build a strong family, it is up to us, as parents, to take our children and direct them specifically towards the things of God. We are called to help prepare our children for their future.

God knew the destiny of your child even before they were conceived in the womb. We have found this to be true for our own children. We caught glimpses of their destiny when they were still in the womb and saw the beginnings of their destiny outworked, even when they were still babies.

A glimpse of destiny

Here are some examples. If we compare our first two children, we saw glimpses of their future destiny emerging long before they could speak. Joshua (the prophetic one) refused to go to strangers. There were very few people who were allowed to hold him except for Mummy, Daddy and a few close friends. But occasionally, when he was a few months old, Joshua would reach out to a complete stranger in church and be happy to be carried by them. After a while we realised that he was reaching out to people who had strong prophetic calls on their lives. On many occasions we would speak to the person Joshua had gone for and ask them if they had a prophetic gift. In every case they had.

"How did you know?" they would ask.

"Joshua, our baby, told us," we would reply, smiling as the bemused stranger tried to work out how our baby had communicated this to us.

So before Joshua could talk, he could recognise the prophetic mantle on the lives of others and felt safe with them.

Our second son, Simeon, has a very different call on his life. He has a pastor's heart. As a young baby he would intentionally reach out for the most hurting, needy and vulnerable members of the church. When we allowed him to go to others he would cuddle right into them. At times adults were moved to tears as they experienced unconditional love from this baby. The difference between the two brothers as young babies was so clear. In both cases the way they reacted was a reflection of their future call.

Sent as a baby

God has a plan for your child. The children that God gives us in these days have a great call on their lives. After all, whenever God sees a need He sends a person as the solution to meet that need.

- When Cain killed Abel, and Adam and Eve needed a godly line, God sent Seth *as a baby*. (Genesis 4 & 5)

- When Abraham needed a successor to fulfil God's promise of becoming a nation He sent Isaac *as a baby*. (Genesis 21:1–5)

- When God saw that the Israelites were suffering in slavery He sent Moses *as a baby*. (Exodus 2:1–2; 3:7–10)

- When Israel needed a judge to go against Philistine oppression He sent Samson *as a baby*. (Judges 13:1–5)

- When God needed a prophet who could speak to the whole nation of Israel He sent Samuel *as a baby*. (1 Samuel 1:11; 19–28)

- When God needed a successor to King David, even though David had sinned with Bathsheba, He gave them Solomon, *as a baby*. (2 Samuel 12:24–25)

- When Israel needed a prophet to speak to the nations in their rebellion, God sent Jeremiah *as a baby*. (Jeremiah 1:5)

- When God needed someone to announce the coming of His Son the Messiah, He sent John the Baptist *as a baby*. (Luke 1:11–16)

- And when God Himself came to earth in human form to save mankind, He did not come as a fully grown adult, but He came *as a baby*. (Luke 1:26–33)

19

As God recorded each of these lives in the Bible, He chose to start their stories from *before* conception or while they were still in the womb. He knew their future calls and planned beforehand the right family and environment for them to be placed in, to prepare them for that call.

Godly parents will train godly children to fulfil God's eternal plans. As you read this book, our desire is that you become empowered to stand alongside other parents of our generation as, together, we prepare the godly army that is needed for our time. May these children rise to be a generation who will "never bow to Baal" (false gods), as God described to Elijah in 1 Kings 19:18. May they be a generation who do not follow the favoured gods of our age, but grow to be a people who know *their* God and do great things for Him.

What is the destiny on your baby's life? Why has God given you this child at this particular time? As their life unfolds, know that God's plans for your child were known before conception, and that the nurturing of their future calling begins from the womb.

God gives children their own angels

> *"Beware that you don't look down on any of these little ones. For I tell you that in heaven their angels are always in the presence of my heavenly Father."*
>
> Matthew 18:10

We always thought that the idea of guardian angels originated in the New Age movement, until we discovered this verse. It states that children have angelic beings who are standing before the throne of the Father. So if children have their own angels, what does this actually mean? Do they have better access to God's presence than us? It would seem to suggest that, but… the answer has to be NO! Anyone who comes to God through Jesus has full and free access to God. Children can't have better access to God than we do, because we already have the best access to God possible—we are called God's children!

So what does it mean?

At the very least it means that God is looking out especially for children. All through the Bible we see that God is interested in how the weakest and most vulnerable members of society are treated by those around them. Children are some of the most vulnerable members of society.

When Jesus walked on the earth He gave children much greater recognition than His disciples thought they deserved. The disciples tried to stop people from bringing their children to Jesus to be blessed, but Jesus rebuked them and blessed the children.

In Luke 18:15, where this particular episode is recorded, Luke does not use the Greek word *paidion* to describe the children, as might have been expected. Instead, he uses the word *brephos*. This word means an unborn or a newborn child. How many pregnant ladies were in the queue pushing forward for Jesus to bless their not-yet-born children? If you were there, wouldn't you have stood in the queue asking Jesus to bless your baby? After all, if Jesus blesses someone, it affects their whole life.

The words of blessing that Jesus spoke over the children were not empty words of well-wishing. Jesus wasn't saying, "Good luck with your life, I hope it all goes okay." Instead He was asking God to bless the children. We know that God answered all of Jesus' prayers, as Jesus didn't do anything unless the Father had first told Him to do it (John 5:19). So these children would be blessed for life, by God, because Jesus had decreed it.

Now imagine if Jesus were to bless your child. Even from the womb they will be blessed for the rest of their lives!

Here then is something practical that we can do to prepare our children for their spiritual future while they are in the womb. We can ask God to bless them. As we take hold of our responsibility to be warriors on behalf of our children, we can start ministering to them in the womb. With God's help, not only will our families be built, but the whole of society will be affected.

As parents we are quick to take notice of the physical health of our children. Let's also take note of their spiritual wellbeing, right from the beginning, making it easier for them to encounter God from the youngest age and live their lives for Him.

For personal reflection

Are you ready to be a warrior for your child?

What is God's destiny on your child?

2

Children in God's Hands

Known before conception?

At what age does God start to interact with a child? As future parents this is a pretty important question for us to answer. If God does not interact with our children until they turn thirteen, then we will be wanting to use their childhood to lay a foundation to prepare for the time when they are old enough to meet with God. If, however, God can interact with them from a young age, even while they are in the womb, then we should be seeking our children to encounter God as soon as possible.

This is indeed the case. In fact, God Himself says that the interaction begins even earlier than conception. Look at His words to the prophet Jeremiah:

> *"I knew you before I formed you in your mother's womb. Before you were born I set you apart and appointed you as my prophet to the nations."*
>
> Jeremiah 1:5

Even before Jeremiah's life began in the womb, God had planned out his life and knew his destiny.

Similarly, the Apostle Paul recognised that God had called him from before birth—even though it took a while for his call to become clear and at times it looked like Saul was doing the exact opposite of what God had planned for him. Nevertheless, God's hand had been on Paul's life, preparing him through circumstances, education, personality, character and connections with people. All these things helped him to fulfil his calling. Paul tells the church in Galatia:

> *"But even before I was born, God chose me and called me by His marvellous grace. Then it pleased Him to*

23

reveal His Son to me so that I would proclaim the
Good News about Jesus to the Gentiles."

Galatians 1:15–16

The prophet Isaiah told a similar story and understood he had
been called to prophetic ministry before he was born:

> *"Listen to me, all you in distant lands! Pay attention,*
> *you who are far away! The Lord called me before my*
> *birth; from within the womb He called me by name."*

Isaiah 49:1

> *"And now the Lord speaks—the one who formed me*
> *in my mother's womb to be His servant, who*
> *commissioned me to bring Israel back to Him. The*
> *Lord has honoured me, and my God has given me*
> *strength."*

Isaiah 49:5

It is clear that God knows the plans He has for each child
before they are born. It is God who creates children in our womb.

> *"Remember the things I have done in the past. For I*
> *alone am God! I am God, and there is none like me.*
> *Only I can tell you the future before it even happens.*
> *Everything I plan will come to pass, for I do whatever*
> *I wish."*

Isaiah 46:9–10

God has made His plans already and He is sending babies into
the world who will grow up to enact and fulfil those plans. Only
God knows the future before it happens. Only He knows the end
from the beginning and He is giving us our children as part of
our heritage in His service.

Dedication before creation

As we have already seen, God has dedicated our children for a
specific purpose. In His plans He has included a human element
in this process of dedication. We see this process at work in the
life of the prophet Samuel. Samuel's mother, Hannah, planned
how she would nurture Samuel before she was even pregnant!
Check out the story:

"Once after a sacrificial meal at Shiloh, Hannah got up and went to pray. Eli the priest was sitting at his customary place beside the entrance of the Tabernacle. Hannah was in deep anguish, crying bitterly as she prayed to the Lord. And she made this vow: 'O Lord of Heaven's Armies, if You will look upon my sorrow and answer my prayer and give me a son, then I will give him back to You. He will be Yours for his entire lifetime, and as a sign that he has been dedicated to the Lord, his hair will never be cut.'

As she was praying to the Lord, Eli watched her. Seeing her lips moving but hearing no sound, he thought she had been drinking. 'Must you come here drunk?' he demanded. 'Throw away your wine!'

'Oh no, sir!' she replied. 'I haven't been drinking wine or anything stronger. But I am very discouraged, and I was pouring out my heart to the Lord. Don't think I am a wicked woman! For I have been praying out of great anguish and sorrow.'

'In that case,' Eli said, 'go in peace! May the God of Israel grant the request you have asked of Him.'

'Oh, thank you, sir!' she exclaimed. Then she went back and began to eat again, and she was no longer sad."

1 Samuel 1:9–28

Samuel was dedicated to God before he was even conceived. His mother's desire was to have a child that would be given over to God. As soon as Samuel was of age, Hannah released him into the care of Eli in the temple. In 1 Samuel 3, Samuel meets God for himself, as a child, when God speaks to him in the night.

Hannah had been desperate for a child. She had longed to have a baby and had cried out to God accordingly. When she finally fell pregnant, you can be sure that this godly woman brought God into her pregnancy. She had already resolved to hand her baby over to God as soon as he was weaned. In the meantime she wouldn't have been ignoring God. Since Hannah had already dedicated her baby to the Lord, this process would have continued throughout the pregnancy, with Hannah praying for him daily. Hannah's dedication and commitment meant that baby Samuel was immersed in the presence of God even before he met God for himself.

From conception onwards Samuel grew into his destiny. God caused him to grow and nurtured him and people noticed it. Everyone saw that there was something special about his life. As Hannah cooperated with God's calling on Samuel, her actions helped to set the divine direction of his life.

Samuel grew up in Eli's household. This home was not the best environment to raise a child in. Even though it was in the temple of God, it was not honouring to God. Eli's sons were wicked men and bad role models for Samuel. Eli himself was a weak father and, though a priest, was lacking in discernment. How else could he have mistaken a distressed woman (Hannah) for a drunkard? Yet, in spite of all of this, Samuel grew to know and serve God.

In 1 Samuel 12:1–3 we read that Samuel was one of the rare people who lived for God all the days of his life. Most of the men and women of God featured in the Bible had their wobbly moments where they doubted God or did not live according to their call. But Samuel lived for God at all times. Even though he'd been put under the care of Eli and had bad role models in the sons of Eli, God's favour was on Samuel's life. Hannah's prayers and her commitment to her son had helped plant a seed in his life that could not be uprooted as he grew older. He remained stable during an unstable time of restructuring in Israel and truly became the voice of God to the people.

So ministry to our children and training of our babies can begin even before a child is in our womb.

If you have already conceived, or already have children, and did not dedicate them to God before birth, don't panic. As we search through the Bible we do not find many things that God commands us to do whilst we are pregnant. Instead, we see signposts, pointing us in the right direction. The suggestions in this book are not things that we have to do to avoid our children running away from God. Rather, they are things that we can do which will benefit our children's life in God.

From all we have seen so far it is clear that:

- God knows children before they are born
- God works on them in the womb
- It is possible for us to dedicate our children to God, even before they are conceived.

Responsive to God in the womb

Whilst God is busy working on our children in the womb to grow them and give them life, do our children have the ability to respond to God?

The Bible answers a resounding YES!

> *"Elizabeth gave a glad cry and exclaimed to Mary, 'God has blessed you above all women, and your child is blessed. Why am I so honoured, that the mother of my Lord should visit me? When I heard your greeting, the baby in my womb jumped for joy. You are blessed because you believed that the Lord would do what He said.'"*
>
> Luke 1:42–45

Elizabeth is pregnant with John the Baptist. She has isolated herself from the rest of the world for a time, as God has given her a child in her old age. This was a divine miracle that involved an angelic visit and the promise that her child would be used by God in the future.

When Mary finds out that she is pregnant an angel tells her that Elizabeth is already in her sixth month of pregnancy—even though everyone thinks she is barren. On hearing this news, Mary hurries to see Elizabeth.

To fully appreciate what is happening when they meet, we need to understand that both these ladies were pregnant with miracle babies of divine promise (one was barren and the other a virgin). We also need to understand two key customs of the day.

Firstly, the mother of a great king or leader would be revered because of their child. The mother of a king would often be given the same honour as the king himself, since she was the one who gave birth, nurtured and prepared him for his future role.

Secondly, in their culture, an older person was always respected by a younger person.

So when the elderly Elizabeth looks at her younger relative, Mary, and describes her as *"the mother of my Lord"* she is breaking the custom of reverence for age and exalting Mary. How did Elizabeth know to do such a dramatic thing? Did an angel visit her to tell her? Had she had a prophetic dream that revealed Mary was pregnant with the Messiah? Where did she get this revelation from that Mary was carrying her Lord?

Verse 44 tells us: *"When I heard your greeting, the baby in my womb jumped for joy."*

This revelation came because of the way her baby moved in the womb. To put it another way, John the Baptist (who was in the 3rd trimester) responded to the Spirit of God in Jesus (1st trimester) in such a way that Elizabeth received revelation.

Many mothers have told me how, when God's presence has been more tangible, they've felt their baby move differently than they normally would. They could recognise when their baby was responding to the Spirit of God and reacting differently. How amazing! It is our privilege and responsibility to nurture this spiritual life.

For Personal Reflection

Take time to dedicate your children to the Lord

3

Nurturing our Babies' Spiritual Lives

We need God

In the previous chapters we have looked at how God interacts with babies in the womb and how they have the potential not only to encounter, but also to respond to, Him. In the light of this, the nurturing of our children's spiritual lives can begin while they are still in the womb.

In spite of all our technological advances, medical breakthroughs and scientific discoveries, every safe birth is still a miracle from God. People can support the process, but it is still God who creates the child in the womb. Once born, we continue to need God to work in us and meet with us so that we can fulfil our destiny.

So what can we do to nurture our babies' spiritual lives whilst they are in the womb?

Based on everything we have been saying we want to suggest four specific, practical things we can do to help our children encounter God while they are in the womb:

1. Offer our child to God
2. Surround our child with the presence of God
3. Pray
4. Speak the right words over our children.

We will look at prayer and the words we speak in chapters 5 and 6. For now let's focus on the first item on our list: offering our children to God.

Offering our child to God

Picture the scene from a Hollywood movie. The new parents take their child to the high priest who then shouts some loud words in a strange tongue while the background music builds to a crescendo and the camera pans around to take in a vast cheering crowd of witnesses. A new baby has been born.

Yet this does not capture the true meaning of dedication. Offering our children to God does not require a fanfare, strange words, orchestral music or even a crowd. Instead it is the heart attitude with which we approach it that counts. Proverbs 22:6 says, *"Direct your children onto the right path, and when they are older, they will not leave it."*

The Hebrew word used for 'direct' here is *chanak*. In different Bible versions the word is variously translated 'train', 'start' or 'raise up'. *Chanak* appears 5 times in the Old Testament and in the other 4 places it is translated as 'dedicate'. In other words, if we dedicate our children to the way they should go, when they are old they will not depart from it.

When objects were dedicated in the temple, it meant that they were presented to God as holy. There were three main steps in dedication:

1. Take the object to the temple

2. Pray over it

3. Leave it in the temple.

If the Assyrians happened to pass by and steal the object, you would chase after them and win it back. When you got it back, the object had to be returned to the temple and rededicated to the Lord to make it holy once again. Such was the importance of dedicated things.

We're not saying you should copy Hannah in 1 Samuel 1:19–28 and drop your baby off at your local church building once he or she is weaned. Your minister would be pretty surprised if everyone turned up with their newly born babies and left him in charge of nursery care and discipleship. But as parents we are responsible for the discipleship of our children and therefore for the process of dedication. Under Jesus, the temple is no longer a physical building, rather it is the place where the Holy Spirit lives.

From all of this we can distil three simple steps to follow to offer our children to God. We should:

1. Bring them into the presence of God
2. Pray over them
3. Leave them in God's presence.

When we offer our children to God we are saying, "God, we want your agenda for our child. We trust you to know what is best for them and know that you will prepare them for their future call. Use us to do our bit for the short time during which you have entrusted them to us as minors. Let us not stand in the way of their call. Instead, we are open to you to use our children however you desire."

This is what the mothers who brought their children to Jesus discovered. They were desperate for Jesus to bless their children, but the disciples thought Jesus had more important things to do. Jesus intervened and told the disciples to let the children come to Him, because the kingdom of God belongs to those who are like children.

Imagine the proud mothers coming forward as the crowd parted in obedience to Jesus so that they could get through. They had fought for the best for their children and now their efforts were about to be rewarded in front of everybody. They expected Jesus to place His hand on the children's head and bless them, as was the custom. What Jesus actually did would have been shocking to them.

"Then he took the children in His arms and placed His hands on their heads and blessed them."

Mark 10:16

Jesus picked the children up in His arms! This is perhaps not surprising to a modern audience, but at the time it was symbolic of adopting a child. Jesus didn't just put His hands on the children and bless them, instead He picked them up in His arms, signifying how important they were—much more than people thought. The parents had brought their children to be blessed, but instead Jesus chose to adopt them, demonstrating the heart of Father God for our children.

As we dedicate our children to God, we are literally trusting Him to be in charge of their lives and to be their guide. By

31

dedicating our children to God we are also offering ourselves to Him, to be used in the shaping and guiding of these children that He has entrusted to us for a time. In short, we are saying to God, "God, this child is Yours to do with as you wish," just like Hannah did with Samuel.

Like Hannah, some women dedicate their children to the Lord when they themselves are young—even before they are married—as a way of saying to God, "Whoever is born from my womb, will be Yours." Others make a conscious effort to offer their children to God during their pregnancy. However we do it, there is something significant about acknowledging that God is in charge of our babies and He has the permission to do whatever He wants with them in His Kingdom.

Surrounding our child with God's presence

A significant part of dedicating our children to God is ensuring that they remain in His manifest presence. While your baby is in your womb they will be wherever you are. If you want your baby to be surrounded by God's presence you will need to ensure that you are! This may sound like one more thing you have to do whilst you are working, cooking and, at times, just tired from being pregnant. So let's break this down a bit more to see how it might work in practice.

Firstly, don't stop going to church. Wherever two or three people gather together, there God is with them. Even though you may be feeling tired and at times won't have the same bounce you once had, perhaps even feeling like Sunday is the one day when you can rest, don't give up meeting with other people who love Jesus. Make a conscious effort to connect with God during the worship and ministry. By all means let your housework slip in exchange for a nap, but keep your spiritual house in order.

Secondly, let worship fill your environment. At home, in the car, at work (if allowed) put on some worship music. For some of the time you may be joining in with the music in worship, but for all of the time your baby will be hearing the music. Choose songs that stir your spirit and your heart towards God and they will have the same effect on your baby.

Thirdly, beware of the mould in the world. Nowadays most women are pretty aware of the health advice to avoid soft cheeses with mould in them. Your immune system can be weaker in pregnancy and the risk of passing on harmful bacteria to your baby is therefore increased. The best thing to do is to avoid the mould in cheeses.

Transfer this principle to your child's spiritual wellbeing and beware of the mould in the world. If you are watching a film, would you want your two-year-old to sit with you while you watched it? If the answer is no, then think carefully about whether you want to expose your unborn child to the same sounds and emotions that the film would evoke in a two year old.

Elizabeth hid herself away when she discovered that she was pregnant with John the Baptist. We are not advocating that you take such extreme measures (after all, we are called to live and interact in this world and frankly if you have a job or this is your second pregnancy it is just not practical), but do apply the test of what you would be willing for your two year old to sit through. Consider what you want your baby to be exposed to.

To put it another way, as you are weighing up what things to listen to, what to watch and where to go, avoid the mould of the world which may be the soft option when you want to relax. Instead, stick to the solid cheddar of God's Spirit. That's the only cheesy part of this book (we promise).

Fourthly, soak your child in prayer. This will be the focus of our next chapter.

As you offer your child to God in your heart and surround them with God's presence in your day, they will begin to connect with God as they grow.

For Personal Reflection

Offer your child to God

Spend time soaking in God's presence

What parts of your life would you not want
your child to be exposed to in the womb?

4

The Importance of Prayer

"Don't worry about anything; instead, pray about everything. Tell God what you need, and thank Him for all He has done. Then you will experience God's peace, which exceeds anything we can understand. His peace will guard your hearts and minds as you live in Christ Jesus."

Philippians 4:6–7

Prayer is the greatest privilege that God has given us. We can talk with the Creator about anything! The good, the bad the indifferent—God knows it all already, so nothing will surprise Him, but He wants us to share with Him. Any friendship involves sharing things. If you do not share with a person, you do not really get to know each other. Matthew 6:8 says, *"Your Father knows exactly what you need even before you ask Him!"*

If God already knows what we need, why do we have to ask? We ask because it shows we trust God to answer and, as we pray, we meet with Him and this changes things on earth. As James says in chapter 5 verse 16, *"The earnest prayer of a righteous person has great power and produces wonderful results."* To put it another way: "When a good man prays, great things happen." God has given us a mandate to govern the earth, so we continue to pray and involve Him in every area of life.

The more we pray, the more we will instinctively involve God in every aspect of our pregnancy. He loves to be involved and as we speak with Him and thank Him, our faith will grow. As we draw nearer to God we will become more accustomed to hearing His voice concerning our pregnancies. This in turn will help us to shut out the voices that are not His. We need God's voice to be the loudest, to drown out what is not of Him, so we will not be hindered in allowing God to be God over our pregnancies.

Look how God links the issues of populating the earth with our children and its governance:

> *"Then God blessed them and said, 'Be fruitful and multiply. Fill the earth and govern it. Reign over the fish in the sea, the birds in the sky, and all the animals that scurry along the ground.'"*
>
> Genesis 1:28

God placed Adam and Eve in charge of the earth. After the fall God did not change His mind; He never took back this authority. We can therefore choose, as humans, who we let be in charge of the world. As we pray we are putting God back in charge. We are letting Him be the master of the world. We are allowing God to act.

James 4:2 says, *"You don't have what you want because you don't ask God for it"* and Luke in chapter 11:9 says, *"And so I tell you, keep on asking, and you will receive what you ask for."* So ask away for the things you would love to happen in your pregnancy.

Make a list and share it with God. Discuss with the Father your hopes and desires for your pregnancy and unborn child. But remember that God's plan happens *"not by force nor by strength, but by My Spirit, says the Lord of Heaven's Armies"* (Zechariah 4:6).

Of course, the best list comes when we start by asking God what His plans are for our child. After all, *"You can make many plans, but the Lord's purpose will prevail"* (Proverbs 19:21).

Pray with your partner

> *"I also tell you this: If two of you agree here on earth concerning anything you ask, My Father in heaven will do it for you."*
>
> Matthew 18:19

Pregnancy requires teamwork. Two become one to form a baby within the womb. As you follow that journey of pregnancy together, prayer will be the key, especially for the husband to feel that he is equally part of what the wife is experiencing. Prayer can help with you both speaking to Father God about your thoughts, feelings and aspirations for your unborn child. It is also the vehicle through which you can pray about any issues that may rise during your pregnancy.

There is power in the two of you praying and agreeing together, speaking to God on behalf of your unborn child, putting God in charge of your pregnancy. Just as a husband will lay his hand on his wife's stomach during pregnancy, so that connection can be made in prayer. During my pregnancies, whenever my husband, Olly, laid his hands on my stomach and prayed, the babies moved. A connection was made between father and baby. The babies felt their father's hand on them and reacted to that as much as John the Baptist reacted to Jesus' presence in the womb. When a godly father speaks words of life, love and destiny into his own children, the children will react.

If your partner is not around or is not following God, then know that God promises to be a Father to the fatherless (Psalm 68:5). His desire is for every child to have a father who will demonstrate something about Father God to them. Where such a role model is not available God promises to fill in the gap in our family unit.

Ask your Dad

One mum who was raising her son on her own taught him that God was his Father. One Christmas he was desperate to have the latest games console. His mum knew that they did not have the money for such an expensive present, so she simply told him to ask his Father. As the boy had done many times before, he went to his room and asked Daddy God for the games console he wanted.

Soon, a friend gave the mum some money. "God told me to give you this for your son's Christmas present," she explained. It was the exact amount needed to buy the games console that he wanted. Daddy God heard and Daddy God provided. He is a Father to the fatherless.

Carry on praying until you get the victory

The prophet Isaiah spoke of how he was going to keep on praying for Jerusalem until he got the results he was looking for.

"Because I love Zion, I will not keep still. Because my heart yearns for Jerusalem, I cannot remain silent. I will not stop praying for her until her righteousness shines like the dawn, and her salvation blazes like a burning torch."

Isaiah 62:1

Praying a prayer of faith and victory shows our confidence in God's word. When the woman with the issue of blood reached out to touch Jesus in Matthew 9, she did so in faith, knowing that she would be healed by that touch. Her faith gave her the strength to push through the crowd to reach Jesus. That faith can be yours when you push through to Jesus in every aspect of your pregnancy.

If you are not happy with the reports from the hospital or the way that you are feeling in your pregnancy, then pray until the victory comes. We will look at this in more detail in chapter 8.

Esther's testimony—supernatural healing

"In my first three pregnancies I had suffered from gestational diabetes. When I became pregnant with my fourth child the doctors told me I would probably get it again. By week 20 I had to start taking insulin and my blood sugar was still not controlled. At this point I started to pray.

"After praying I felt that God had healed me. I stopped taking my insulin by faith and carefully monitored my sugar levels which started to balance out. They were higher with the insulin than without it!

"By the next day my sugar levels became normal, so I went to the hospital to let them know I had stopped the insulin. They tested me and all the results came back normal. My baby even returned to the normal size!

"The consultant and the diabetic nurse both wrote in my notes that it was due to my prayers. They had no medical explanation for these changes. Baby James was born after four strong contractions with no sugar issues and I continue to be well."

Often, when there is a battle in the spiritual realm, we can come up against a blockage in prayer. It is then that we, as parents, need to stand strong and be stubborn in prayer for our unborn children. The saying, "If you are finding it hard to pray, pray harder" is a great encouragement to keep on pressing into God, until we either understand His plan in the middle of the situation or see the situation change to match His plan. It is through prayer that we can stand against the fears inside us and negative reports from others around us.

Prayer is not a magic button to make things happen. Rather, it is a button of faith that activates trust in God, knowing that He knows best in our circumstances and that through prayer He will bring about His best for us. As Spurgeon said, "Prayer is the slender nerve that moves the hand of God." Stand as a woman of faith on behalf of your child no matter what the circumstances around you. God is a God who hears and understands.

Prayer soaking for pregnant mums

"Be still and know that I am God."

Psalm 46:10

"Be still before the Lord and wait patiently for Him."

Psalm 37:7

"Jesus said to them, 'Come with me by yourselves to a quiet place and get some rest.' So they went to a solitary place."

Mark 6:31–32

Ladies, here is a way that you can make prayer a priority throughout your pregnancy. This can be done on your own, with a few friends, other church members or other pregnant ladies.

Set aside time to be still before God. You can adopt whatever position you feel most comfortable in for your stage of pregnancy and just welcome God to come by His Holy Spirit and speak to you. We have produced a soaking CD for pregnant women to accompany this book which you can use in your times of soaking.

This is a great time not just to talk to God, but to listen to Him and hear what He would like to say to you personally or through another person. Prayer is a two-way process and God loves it when we allow Him time to speak into our lives and those of our unborn children.

These times can open the floodgates to God speaking to us, while He has our attention. When we are still, simply acknowledging and aware of God's presence, an exciting time of communication can begin. As you sit you can think about some of the verses at the start of this section.

"Be still and know that I am God."

Psalm 46:10

Make notes of the prayers afterwards for you to meditate on during your pregnancy.

Keep a prayer journal and prayer notebook

As you listen to God for your child, He will speak to you, either directly by His Spirit, through His Word or through other people. When God spoke to Mary, and when other people told her what God had revealed to them, we read that,

"Mary kept all these things in her heart and thought about them often."

Luke 2:19

Nine months disappears fast when you are pregnant and remembering what God has said to you for your unborn child can easily be forgotten. But if you keep a prayer journal during this time you will be constantly reminded of the things you are bringing to God in persistent prayer and can give thanks as you look back at how He answered. Here are some of the things you may want to write in the journal:

- A letter to God to express yourself and the way you are feeling at various times of your pregnancy
- Words of prophecy over your unborn child
- A list of concerns to be prayed through
- Answers to prayers that you have prayed
- A record of significant moments during the pregnancy
- Bible passages that help you to focus on God being at the centre of pregnancy.

The more you refer to this journal and record the testimonies of how you have seen God answer prayer, the more your faith will rise, knowing God is control of your pregnancy and your unborn child's destiny. We have produced a prayer journal for use during pregnancy that you may find a helpful resource as you prepare for your child. The things you write in your journal at this time are things you can treasure as your child grows through different seasons and on into adulthood.

Ask others to pray for you

As well as having a baby shower, why not hold a prayer shower where people come to pray and prophesy over your baby? You can invite people round to your house to worship with you and pray for you, but choose the people carefully.

1 Timothy 5:22 says, *"Do not lay hands on anyone hastily, nor share in other people's sins; keep yourself pure."*

This implies that there is a transference of nature when people lay hands on us. Choose people who are godly in character and full of the Holy Spirit to come and lay hands on your baby. You want people who you can trust and who are in tune with God's voice.

Karis' story—God's protected labour

"I was 26 and Guy was 27 when we discovered, a little sooner than planned, that we were expecting our first baby. Naturally, we prayed for this little person growing inside of me over the busy months, but to be honest, feeling young and invincible, this was quite sporadic as we got on with things like buying our first home and settling into new jobs. We had just returned to South Africa after a year of travelling.

"By the time I was 33 weeks, the pregnancy was progressing according to plan. We had sort of decorated most of our newly acquired flat and were beginning to think about the nursery. One morning I went off to work as usual but by midday was feeling really tired. I'd had a meeting close to home so went home to get lunch. I ended up sleeping for two hours and when I awoke I noticed my ankles were very swollen.

"This was the first time this had happened to me, but I knew it was a normal part of pregnancy, so I wasn't too bothered by it. Later, I fetched Guy from work and, hoping to improve my circulation, we went for a lovely walk along the beachfront on the way home. When we got home I said I thought I would miss our church home group as I still felt weary, but Guy was having none of it and off we went.

"We had only been attending our group for about six months. It was quite a quiet group and we were the youngest by a fair bit. Half way through the evening one of the women, out of the blue, said she felt we should pray for me and the baby. In a way that was uncharacteristic for that group, she got me to stand in the middle while they all laid hands on me and my tummy and prayed.

"The prayers were for my baby who had been knit together in my womb, that she would know and love God, and for strength and health for me and the babe and for God's protection and safety during the weeks ahead. The baby kicked those who had placed hands on my tummy as we finished praying, which made us laugh, and we left with an amazingly tangible sense of God's love and protection.

"That night I slept fitfully and woke at 4:45 a.m. thinking my waters had broken. When I got to the toilet I realised that I was bleeding. I called for Guy who I remember immediately knelt down next to me and began to call on God. We then stopped praying and phoned our doctor.

"My placenta had ruptured. A few hours later after a general anaesthetic and an emergency caesarean we had a tiny baby girl. I had been very small and people had barely started to notice I was pregnant, so the hospital staff later said they had been really worried as to how the baby would be, yet she was exactly the right weight for 33 weeks at 2 kg or 4.4 pounds.

"We still had a dicey period where the paediatrician would not make any promises, but we knew that God was with us in a most amazing way. So many miraculous things fell into place over that week. It was a period of our life that despite, or perhaps because of, the unbelievable anxiety coupled with our naiveté, we look back and absolutely know God's presence and sovereignty.

"The thing that stays with me is how often we pray for protection and don't know what could have been without those prayers. But in this instance it was so tangible. Much later the doctor advised me not to go and read up on all the things that can go wrong with both mother and baby when the placenta ruptures, but we hold on to the fact that those remarkable prayers covered us.

"Our daughter, Antonia, is now 19 and loves and serves God wonderfully, working with children and teenage girls at church, in summer conferences, and presently in her workplace as assistant chaplain in a secondary school."

Ask people to lay hands on your belly and pray for your child. Receive any prophetic words God may have for you. Don't forget to keep a record of anything significant that people say—you may use it to encourage yourself and others in the future.

I don't know what to pray for my unborn child

You may already be deep in prayer for your child, raising specific desires or concerns to God. Alternatively, you may have tried to pray, but didn't really know where to begin. It may even be that the whole concept of prayer is new to you. Put simply, prayer is about talking with God. Act like you are talking to your friend. God isn't into airs and graces. He doesn't care if you are not the most eloquent person in the world. All He cares about is your relationship with Him.

I used to go on walks with God in the woods and talk out loud and openly to Him as if I had a friend beside me, just chatting. If someone else came walking up the path I would stop talking so they didn't think I was crazy! But now people talk on the phone all the time through wireless headpieces, so if you do this and someone does overhear you talking, they will probably just assume you're on the phone to someone. And in a way you are—you're using your hotline to God.

If you are struggling to find some words to pray the Bible is full of prayers. If you turn to Psalms there are many to choose from. Just pray a psalm over yourself and your unborn child's life. Alternatively, look up the words to an old hymn and speak them over your child. Many have profound and powerful lyrics that are in themselves prayers to God.

Towards the end of this book you will also find some declarations that you can pray over your child, based on the Scriptures. We encourage you to use these declarations as you pray.

The prayer of praise and thanksgiving

Finally, in all things, praise the Lord. When we praise and thank God it brings us into His wonderful presence. Why not set up a thanksgiving board in your kitchen or another suitable area in your home, where you can pin up things you want to say "thank you" to God for. Write down Bible passages on a piece of card to meditate on and use in praise.

Even if negative things happen or negative words are spoken regarding your pregnancy and unborn child, praising God at a time when praise seems like the last thing we want to do is incredibly powerful: it affirms our faith and trust in God. This is a powerful weapon. Satan hates praise, since he was once in charge of it and that was taken away from him. The power of praise takes down anything Satan may want to form against us, in our thought life or even our physical life.

Sing until you can sing no more and thank God for the wonderful child He is giving you. Be grateful in all things. As God's Word declares, *"Let everything that breathes sing praises to the Lord!"* (Psalm 150:6)

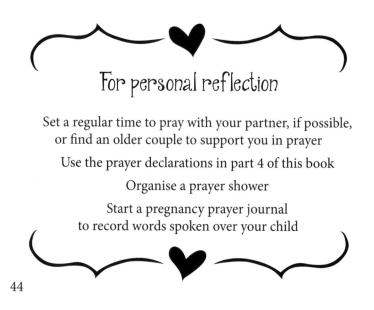

For personal reflection

Set a regular time to pray with your partner, if possible, or find an older couple to support you in prayer

Use the prayer declarations in part 4 of this book

Organise a prayer shower

Start a pregnancy prayer journal
to record words spoken over your child

5

The Power of Words

*"As he considered this, an angel of the Lord appeared
to him in a dream. 'Joseph, son of David,' the angel
said, 'do not be afraid to take Mary as your wife. For
the child within her was conceived by the Holy
Spirit. And she will have a son, and you are to name
him Jesus, for He will save His people from their sins.'"*

Matthew 1:20–21

The meaning of a name

Many people choose names for their children before they are
born. People choose those names for all kinds of reasons.
Some choose names that are popular, according to the latest
trend or just because they sound nice. Others spend time looking
into the meanings of names.

The meanings of names can be important. One church called
themselves 'The Ichabod Fellowship' because it was biblical.
Unfortunately, they hadn't checked the meaning of the word
'Ichabod' carefully enough. 1 Samuel 4:21 tells us that it means, 'The
glory has departed'! Is this a church you would want to attend?

Throughout the Bible, we see that the names of people have
great meaning and are often tied in with their destiny.

God wanted to bless all nations through a man called Abram
and give him countless descendants. To seal the deal God gave
Abram a new name, a new identity and an amazing life-changing
promise. In itself, Abram was a great name, meaning 'exalted
father', which spoke of how Abram was respected by those
around him. But it did not fit his future destiny. Now God was
promising Abram that he would be the 'father of many'. God
changed his name to Abraham, meaning 'father of many' to
reflect this.

At the time, however, this 'father of many' had *no* children! Can you imagine Abraham breaking the news to his friends?

"Hey Abram, how are you doing? Do you fancy a cappuccino?"

"Listen guys, I've been wanting to speak to you about something. The thing is, God's spoken to me and I've got a new name. From now on, please call me Abraham. I'm going to be the father of whole nations."

"Umm, Abe…"

"It's Abraham."

"Okay, Abra-ham. We know you have Ishmael, so we pray that God will make him into a nation."

"No," Abraham replies, sweating slightly. "Ishmael doesn't count in this. God's going to give Sarah and me a son together."

"Do you mean Sarai, your wife?"

"Yup, but God changed her name too. She's now 'Sarah.'"

"Okay Abe," his friends say, glancing at their mobile phones, desperately thinking how they can change the subject; wondering how they might get a psychiatric assessment for their friend and his 90-year-old barren wife. They are clearly losing the plot…

But they weren't losing the plot. They were taking hold of what God had spoken regarding their destiny and speaking it out. Acknowledging their new names, their new identities, was an important part of this.

In the Bible, God has many titles or names, each one revealing a different aspect of His character. Similarly, when God gave people names, each had a significant meaning. Even the names that God didn't give to people directly had a meaning.

Moses' name was given to him as a way of explaining how he was found in the river. His adoptive mother drew him out of the river and his name literally means, 'to draw out'. It also spoke of his destiny and the call of his life, which was to 'draw out' God's people from Egyptian slavery and lead them into the Promised Land.

Other names revealed the parents' reaction to the birth of their child. Isaac means 'laughter', because Sarah reacted with both joy and disbelief at becoming a mother when she thought she could not.

In 1 Chronicles 4:10 Jabez, whose name means 'pain', cried out to God that his life would not be defined by the label his parents had given him.

As we move into the New Testament, the meaning of names is still important as it was in the Old Testament. In Luke 1:13 God told Zechariah that he should call his son John, which means 'Yahweh is gracious'. His destiny would be to turn many of Israel back to God and the hearts of fathers to their children. This was not a name that was common in Zechariah's or Elizabeth's families (Luke 1:61), so it was not the kind of name people would have expected them to pick. But this was a sign of God's destiny on John's life.

When the fisherman Simon started to follow Jesus, Jesus changed his name to fit his newly uncovered destiny: he would be Peter, meaning 'rock'. Peter, as one of the key apostles, would be a rock in the early Church.

The meaning of Jesus' name had great significance too. The name Jesus literally means 'the Lord saves'. This was the very purpose of His life: to save people from their sins.

Today many believers around the world change their name when they come to Jesus as a sign of the change He has brought about in them and as a statement, putting behind them their lives prior to knowing Christ.

Prophetic names

The names we give our children are labels by which they will be known and called. That makes them important. After all, Proverbs 18:21 tells us that, *"The tongue can bring death or life."* This does not mean that names are a magic spell that will change their destiny. If you call your daughter Violet, she will not turn a deep shade of purple because of it! But at the same time, let's not go to the other extreme and say that their name has no significance at all. If that were the case, God would not be in the business of changing people's names.

One of the greatest joys (and sometimes one of the most hotly debated discussions) we have as parents is choosing what we will call our children once they are born. But there is a more pressing challenge that we have to address first. What should we call them while they are in the womb? Should they be called 'it', as some suggest, which implies they are not yet human? Should we refer to them using the generic 'he', even though they may actually be a 'she'? Should we avoid labelling their gender before it's known and go for the non-specific 'they'? (We tried this once and had many people wondering if we were going to give birth to twins or even quadruplets!) Perhaps we could adopt a nickname for them: 'Bump', 'Plum' or 'Little 'un'?

So many choices. But if God sees the naming of things as both important and something that we can do (Adam's first official job title was 'chief namer-of-animals' in the garden of Eden, before he was demoted to general farm labourer) then perhaps we should give a bit more thought to the name we call our unborn children while they are in the womb.

How powerful would it be if we gave our unborn child a prophetic name in the womb? A label from God that spoke into their destiny. God already knows that destiny, just like He knew what He was calling Jeremiah to be before He even formed him in the womb (Jeremiah 1:5).

For each of our children we prayed and sought God for a name to call them whilst they were in the womb. So instead of people coming up to us and pointing to 'bump' and asking, "How is 'the baby'?" we had 9 months of people declaring words of life and destiny over our children, through the names God had given us.

These names were strictly just for whilst they were in the womb. Then, of course, we asked God to give us their lifetime names too. With each of our children, God has honoured the womb names He gave us as each child has grown to live up to the name they were given.

Birth name: *Joshua* meaning *God is Salvation.*
Womb name: *Blessed and Beloved.* This boy is so loved by all who meet him. He lights up a room when he walks in and

people love having him around. He is blessed in so many ways, in fact the first time we ever had to buy him any clothes was when he was 5 years old and that was a pair of pyjamas. Up until then people kept blessing him with clothing. (In fact, the day after we bought him those pyjamas another pair arrived in the post, sent by some friends!) Joshua is continually blessed in so many ways.

Birth name: *Simeon* meaning *He has heard.*
Womb name: *Grace and Favour.* Simeon has so much favour wherever he goes. People gather around him and he has so much grace for everyone. He is a very giving child, always giving and accepting other people. He has a real pastoral heart towards people—a big heart of care and love. He constantly surprises us at the grace he exhibits to others and the level of deep thought he puts into what others are feeling.

Birth name: *Matthew* meaning *Gift of God.*
Womb name: *Jubilee, Destiny.* The name Jubilee comes from the Jewish calendar. Every seven years the Jews were told to take a year of rest—a Sabbath year. After every seventh Sabbath year they were to take an extra year of rest, during which they were to release any Israelite slaves and hand back any property or land they had bought from fellow Israelites. Other than land in the city, you could not sell your land to other people. Instead you could only lease the land for the number of years that were remaining until the year of Jubilee. We chose the name Jubilee because, as we prayed for our unborn Matthew, we felt God saying He would use Matthew as an evangelist to restore people to Jesus.

Birth name: *Benjamin* meaning *Son of my right hand.*
Womb name: *Faithful Jewel.* When we started praying for a prophetic womb name for Benjamin we received the name 'Obedient Servant'. He would faithfully follow God as an obedient servant follows his master. As we thought about this name, we realised that it could easily be misunderstood by others, who would be calling him that name for the next 9 months. We imagined our friends saying to us, "So basically you want him to be a household slave to you both?" We

thought and prayed some more and realised that every person who loves to serve in the body of Christ is a faithful jewel in God's Kingdom. We had found his prophetic name. Benjamin loves to help in the home in any way he can and at the age of five is already exhibiting his servant heart. He diligently helps with little jobs, with a skip in his step. He loves life, loves serving and does it all with such joy.

Birth name: *Abigail* meaning *Father's rejoicing.*
Womb name: *Godly Example.* We felt this little girl would be an amazing role model to all those around her; that people would look to her as a godly example to know how to act. She is already a great role model in crèche, where she kisses and hugs all the children who are crying and loves those who are on their own.

We have heard of lots of other names that people have given their unborn child. One that made us chuckle was when a friend called her unborn child 'Goodness and Mercy'. We joked that "Goodness and Mercy will follow her all the days of her life."

"If only you knew how prophetic that ended up being for the first few years of her life," the mum told us recently, since her clingy daughter wanted to follow her everywhere.

Laura's testimony—a name we needed

Laura, a first time mother, says how the prophetic name she and her husband gave to their baby had great meaning to them once the baby was born.

"During my pregnancy we prayed for a prophetic name for our baby. We felt God gave her the name Victory. When she was born we named her Eliza Wren. Four days after her birth Eliza was readmitted to hospital with jaundice. Her bilirubin levels were so high that the doctors said she would need a blood exchange. There was talk of neurological damage if the levels weren't brought down quickly.

"During this time our initial response was to worry. We were scared for her future. But as we prayed God reminded us of her womb name: 'Baby Victory'. God assured us that she would have victory over this illness.

"In the days that followed she recovered fully. She responded so quickly to light therapy that she didn't need the blood exchange. The doctors were amazed at her rapid recovery.

"I took longer to recover from it all. The shock had knocked my confidence and with Eliza needing advanced hearing tests and a 6-week check with the consultant to ensure the levels had not damaged her brain, I could feel myself beginning to get anxious. Again, during prayer, God reminded me of the name He had given her in the womb and showed me that I needed to not only hold on to this for the current situation, but to trust Him and live a victorious life myself—fully relying on Him and knowing that when challenges come, I have the victory in Him.

"Eliza is, of course, perfect and through her prophetic name she truly won the battle and lived up to that name—even in the very early stages of her life."

All of this name calling is more than just assigning an appropriate name. It is a process through which we want to hear from God about our child's calling. God already knows their divine destiny and often He is willing to share it with us. We encourage you seek God for your child's destiny and call them a prophetic name while they are in the womb.

Negative words over the womb

> *"The real art of conversation is not only to say the right thing at the right time, but to leave unsaid the wrong thing at the tempting moment."—Dorothy Nevill*

It's amazing, as a mother-to-be, how many throw away comments one can receive, negatively predicting how your child is going to turn out:

"Enjoy being pregnant while you can… it's all downhill from there."

"Just you wait till they are two. The tantrums will start and then you will have your hands full."

"Don't wish their life away too quickly. The teenage years will kick in and that's when the rebellion starts."

Or for me, "Wow! You have four boys and a girl? You're brave, they must be a real handful!"

These spoken words hang over our children, trying to shape their destiny. Words are powerful, but as parents we have the authority to decide whether or not we receive them. Numbers 30 in the Bible points to this principle. If a person makes a foolish vow on behalf of their family, and their partner doesn't act to correct it, then the vow stands. If they reject the vow, then it becomes invalid. In other words, we have authority over what we allow into our home or to influence our family.

James 3 speaks about the power of the tongue. James describes the tongue like the rudder of a ship, which can either steer into danger or into safety. Our words set the direction for our life; that is how powerful they are. The words we speak matter. They not only reveal what is in our heart (see Luke 6:45 and Proverbs 4:23), but they also speak to our destiny.

When we speak God's word over a situation, those words carry even more authority. God never speaks empty words; His words have power! He spoke and the world was created. Now the words He speaks continue to do the job that He sends them to do. As Isaiah 55:10–11 says:

> *"As the rain and the snow come down from heaven,*
> *and do not return to it without watering the earth*
> *and making it bud and flourish, so that it yields*
> *seed for the sower and bread for the eater, so is My*
> *word that goes out from My mouth: It will not return*
> *to Me empty, but will accomplish what I desire and*
> *achieve the purpose for which I sent it."*

Whenever we speak God's Word into a circumstance then God is in that circumstance! Our words carry immense power. Our words also show what we are focussing on. If our child throws a tantrum as a toddler, the words we use in response will either give attention to that or take attention away from it. It is easy as parents to focus on ten minutes of negative or poor behaviour from our children and miss the 23 hours and 50 minutes of wonderful behaviour they've shown. It is important that we keep things in perspective because, handled badly, those 10 minutes can spread like a cancer in our child's life. If we continually speak to them and others about their tantrums, it can become a self-fulfilling prophecy. Instead, if we focus on and speak about all their good behaviour, our words will strengthen this aspect of their character.

Our children will likely go through seasons of carelessness or have tantrums. This does not mean that this is who they are! They don't need to rebel as a teenager. There may be days in your life where you feel your children are a handful, but if that is the direction in which you are thinking, rather than looking at the positives, then certainly it will be easier for the negatives to wear down you and your family.

I remember once being in the lower hall of our church as I was carrying my newborn, Joshua, around in my sling. Different people were speaking to me and it felt as though an onslaught of well-meaning but negative comments were coming at me, regarding my son's future life. Many were said in a tongue-in-cheek way, or in an 'advisory' capacity, but nevertheless, they went against my hopes, dreams and aspirations for my son.

It is easy for careless words spoken by others to hang over our children's lives like curses—like the vows which, if not revoked, remain intact. If we accept these as normal, rather than declaring the words of God and prophesying words of truth and godly destiny over our children, they we have already succumbed to the world's view of children. We are not naïve, believing that as we prophesy God's best for our children that they will become the perfect children. We all enter this world as sinners! Yet, as parents, we are the gatekeepers for our children and recognise that spoken words carry power. We all know that the playground nursery rhyme, *Sticks and stones may break my bones, but words will never hurt me*, is simply not true.

Let's reach for God's best for our children, even though sin is in their fallen nature. We are not saying we should ignore their wrong behaviour. Of course this should be dealt with at the time it happens. Rather we are highlighting the need for vigilance regarding the words we speak over our children, and the words of others that we allow to *remain* over their lives. Even on a psychological level, if we focus on the good in our children and speak this out, this will define their perception of themselves. How much more can affect their lives for good when we consider the added spiritual dimension of the authority and responsibility God has given us over our children, to shape their destinies and prepare them for their future calling.

Why don't you set some time aside now on your own, or with your partner, to ask God what He would like to speak over your unborn child? Discover what prophetic name you can call them while they are in the womb.

As you focus on this, remember a word from God does not return empty but achieves its purpose. This is the start of words of blessing and destiny touching your child's life and the power of God's blessing is phenomenal!

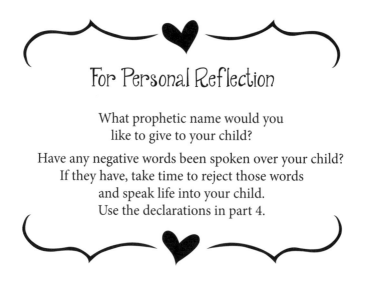

For Personal Reflection

What prophetic name would you
like to give to your child?

Have any negative words been spoken over your child?
If they have, take time to reject those words
and speak life into your child.
Use the declarations in part 4.

6

Not What I Expected

Karen's story—I wasn't ready for this child

"When I was pregnant with my third son, he was unplanned and I was unprepared. At the time, my two youngest children were aged 4 and 2 and it was a season of my life which was extremely stressful. I made God very aware of how I was feeling. How could I be pregnant AGAIN?!

"I spiralled into a depressive state, mainly because there was a close family member of mine who wasn't able to have children. She desperately wanted a child, but hadn't had any. Why was God giving me so many children when my family member had none? I was not praying for more children and was taking appropriate precautions, yet this close family member was praying hard to have one child. It was a really, really dark season for me.

"I know that there are other women who are currently going through what I went through and don't want to be pregnant. All around me people were doing the usual, such as saying 'Congratulations!' or 'You must be so excited!' or asking, 'Do you know what you're having?' People would also come up to me and quote every child-related scripture there is, and I was just not interested. But, God was faithful. If this is what you are going through, just hold on and do what you know to do, even if your emotions are not engaged. Trust God to bring you through it, because He will.

"Meanwhile, I was having an internal breakdown. I couldn't conceive how I would mentally cope with three children all under the age of five. This was despite having a loving husband, a supportive family and phenomenal friends. The tunnel ahead, in my opinion, was long and dark with no light in sight.

"BUT GOD…!

"For about six months I don't think I spoke to God, apart from complaining and criticising. Some Christians (the really holy and perfect ones) will be appalled by this confession. But the truth is, I was so disappointed, mainly with myself, that I had nothing to say to God. So I said nothing. I was just doing the 'Mother thing' in terms of praying blessings for protection over my unborn child, but I wasn't having the communion with God that I'd had up until then.

"Then my family member called me one day and she said to me, 'I need you to be praying over that child'. I told her, 'I am not even in a frame of mind to pray', so she said she would write a prayer and wanted me to read it over the child. (You will find a similar prayer in part 4 of this book). That is what I did, literally and methodically, every day. I wasn't even engaged in the process, but God is so faithful. We serve an awesome God who knows where we are at and sees us through the dark times. He really did that for me.

"One day while washing the dishes, looking out the window, doing what I did best at that time—complaining—God made a statement that got my attention immediately. He said to me, 'Karen, things could be much worse. I could take away the two you have.' It was at that exact moment that I saw the light. WOW! He was right. This was not the worst thing that could happen to me—as I had been telling myself—things could be much worse!

"It was at that moment that things began to change. God began to soften my heart, change my mind and ultimately transform my life. My attitude changed and everything began to follow suit.

"Today, I call my son my 'Dare-to-Dream baby'. He was the baby that became my turning point and is a constant reminder that even in the midst of our madness (sometimes self-imposed) our God is faithful."

Negative thoughts towards our unborn babies

Wouldn't it be great if life was like a fairy tale? Everything would be perfect. We would be the perfect parents and feel perfectly fulfilled at all times. This is the image that advertising companies attempt to sell to new parents.

Cue the TV advert of the smiling, pregnant lady, rubbing her pregnant tummy with a combined look of hope, peace and joy, as her adoring, handsome husband looks on from behind. Switch scenes to the mother looking glamorous as she changes her baby's nappies while they interact together. Add in a quick close up of the giggling baby, now zoom back out to see the joyous interaction one more time. Note that it is always daytime in these adverts, because advert babies don't wake up in the middle of the night. The sun is always shining, the mum has had time to apply a perfect layer of makeup, both mother and baby's clothes are always clean and the house is always tidy and clutter free.

This is the expectation that the world puts on us and, indeed, is the aspiration most parents want to achieve. The reality can be far from this picturesque ideal. All kinds of feelings can be stirred up whilst the hormones are flying around, ranging from mild uncertainty about the future through to outright rejection of the baby.

- What affect will this baby have on my career?
- How will we cope financially?
- What will the birth be like?
- How will my marriage cope with this added pressure?
- Will I be a good mum?
- Why did I have to fall pregnant at this time?

We may know that some of these thoughts are wrong and so try to bury them or deny their existence, instead of challenging them head on. If we allow such thoughts to go round our heads unchallenged, we instinctively know this cannot be good for our baby, but the truth is: it will pull us down too.

Paul instructs us in 1 Corinthians 10:5 to take captive every thought. This means we should challenge thoughts that are contrary to God's Word and plan—and His plan is always good.

In Jeremiah 29:11 God says: *"For I know the plans I have for you. They are plans for good and not for disaster, to give you a future and a hope."* God is the giver of life and if you are pregnant it is He who has given you your child. The Psalmist writes in Psalm 127 verse 3, *"Children are a gift from the Lord; they are a reward from Him."*

If you are weighed down by negative thoughts towards your baby, fight these thoughts, trusting that God is over all the details. If the feelings are too strong to fight, share them with someone. You are not alone. Work with God to change your thinking.

One lady was busy writing a book as a camera crew filmed her family. At least, she was *trying* to write her book… her children kept interrupting her. The producer asked her, "Doesn't it annoy you having all these interruptions while you are trying to write your book?" She replied, "The children are not the interruption, the book is."

Think of the impact those words, and the heart attitude behind them, will have on her children. Her children are more important to her than the day-to-day running of the household or the writing of a book. In the midst of her busyness they still mattered.

The words and actions of a mother make her children feel secure in who they are. I would like to say that I react like this constantly, but I don't. I have to constantly remind myself to build up and not tear down my children. If we can focus on the fact that our children are a God-given blessing to us, then we have started to realise the miracle and privilege of raising children.

One lady said to me, "I think the biggest thing I wish I'd done is trust my child to God whilst they were still in the womb, as I'd have worried far less. The kids were 1 and 4 by the time I did! I would also have prayed for them *in utero* far more than I did." That's the benefit of hindsight! Let her hindsight be your foresight.

An unborn baby is affected deeply by the attitudes of the mother. If the mother rejects the child in her womb, the child can suffer from this rejection later on in life. Hence the womb is a seat of influence. The right time to tackle wrong attitudes towards our unborn children is before they are born.

For Personal Reflection

If you are struggling with a negative attitude
towards your baby:

Decide you want to change your attitude

Start to read the declarations
in part four of this book

Confide in a close Christian friend
and ask them to pray for you

Trust that the same God who put this new life in you
has worked out all the details along the way,
even if you don't see how it is going to work out

7

Combatting Fear

Facing fear

"Don't be afraid, for I am with you. Don't be discouraged,
for I am your God. I will strengthen you and help you.
I will hold you up with My victorious right hand."

Isaiah 41:10

It is perfectly normal to feel some form of fear or anxiety during pregnancy. Your hormones are changing and your body is changing in a way that it never has and never will do again, except in pregnancy. As a new life grows inside you, you can feel as if you are losing control of your life. When even simple tasks like putting on shoes require a pre-arranged action plan, it's no wonder we have to work harder than normal to *"lead every thought and purpose away captive into the obedience of Christ (the Messiah, the Anointed One)"* (2 Corinthians 10:5 AMP) and to *"set our minds and keep them set on what is above (the higher things), not on the things that are on the earth"* (Colossians 3:2 AMP).

If you have tried for years to conceive, some of these fears may be brought on due to the fact that you are desperate that nothing goes wrong for your special little one. Some ladies may have experienced the loss of miscarriage and, as I have experienced, the attachment you have made to your little baby in the womb, right from that positive pregnancy test onward, is very strong. To have our child taken away from us without, in some cases, any explanation is heart breaking, but also makes us even more concerned for our next pregnancy, that it won't happen again. Fears for our health, our family situation or the future can all try hang on to us.

But although fear for your child may try to hold on to you, those feelings of anxiety for your baby show that you have already developed that undeniable love for your unborn child, wanting the best for them right from the start. For some ladies, that feeling of love comes a little later, whilst they are trying to get their heads around what is happening to them—but it will come.

God doesn't want us to feel fear. In John 8:36 we read that, *"If the Son sets you free, you are truly free."* Freedom is what you need to fulfil your destiny and that freedom comes from God.

Rachel—change my attitude

"With my second pregnancy, I wish I had walked with my head high instead of down. I had twin toddler boys at the time who were full of mischief and I looked very young. I always felt people were judging me for being pregnant again, especially as we lived in a town with lots of teenage pregnancies. I felt like people were looking at me in that way. I struggled big time with the fear of what other people were thinking.

"Something changed when I became pregnant with my fourth child. Now my mentality was, 'I have chosen to have these children.' I am proud to have these young children and am not ashamed. My way of thinking really changed how I coped practically too."

Fighting fear

> *"For God has not given us a spirit of fear and timidity, but of power, love, and self-discipline."*
>
> 2 Timothy 1:7

We have to fight in order to have freedom. We need to fight against our fears, knowing that fear does not come from God. Fear is a weapon of the enemy, designed to make us question God's character. Satan's biggest weapon is his words. Just as faith comes by hearing (Romans 10:17) so does fear. This is Satan's earliest trick: "Did God really say…?" He questions us and tries to put "what ifs" into our thoughts. But all the devil has is his roar. We have God on our side to help us through.

We need to put empowering thoughts into our mind. As my friend Melissa says, "Your child is not doomed if your pregnancy and birth don't conform to the way things are 'supposed' to happen."

God has called us to have a fear-free life. A good explanation of FEAR, using an acronym, is False Evidence Appearing Real.

Fear is worrying about a situation or circumstance that hasn't actually happened in reality. When we are filled with fear, the remedy is to be filled with God's love, because *"perfect love expels all fear"* (1 John 4:18) and *"God is love"* (1 John 4:8). A perfect revelation of God will remove the need for fear.

If you are facing fears turn to part 4. Here you will find a list of specific fears, with some practical pointers and prayers to pray to combat the fear. Turn your fears into FAITH: Firmly And Intimately Trusting Him.

Above all know that God *is* in control.

Michelle and Charles' testimony—freedom from fear

"Most people I knew had had terrible experiences of childbirth. Because of this I had a longstanding fear of childbirth. I went to a womb ministry meeting where one of the midwives explained that God has programmed us so that when we relax, we produce hormones that make baby's delivery easy, whilst fear and anxiety produces the opposite result. This simple truth stuck in my mind.

"The more I learnt about pregnancy and childbirth the better prepared I felt. It was so amazing how much knowing about childbirth—and especially knowing God's mind set for pregnancy and delivery—made a difference to our lives. We prayed through scriptures and confessed them over our family regularly. As we did this, my mind set changed until we knew, beyond any reasonable doubt, that God was in control of everything concerning the birth of our baby.

"The delivery of our first child, Deborah, was such a wonderful experience; no fear! We were so relaxed and in control throughout the not-so-painful, short and easy labour, that it felt like a short trip to the hospital and back. We were so happy. We couldn't believe that was it.

"Now we know and believe that in everything we do in life our mind set is important. If we let God put things in the right order in our mind, it will make a huge difference to the way things are accomplished in our lives. For me, the biggest fear of my life turned out to be the biggest victory. Thanks be to God!"

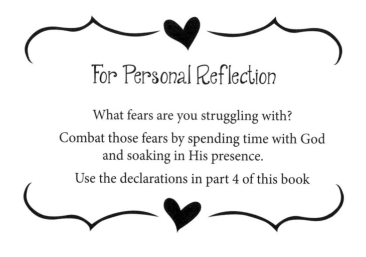

For Personal Reflection

What fears are you struggling with?

Combat those fears by spending time with God and soaking in His presence.

Use the declarations in part 4 of this book

8

Vigorous Women

What kind of woman do you want to be?

In Exodus 1:15–21 the story of the Hebrew midwives is told. The king of Egypt had ordered these midwives to kill every male child who was born, but they feared God and refused to follow through on this command. When the king summoned them wanting to know why they were not following orders they had an easy reply to give him: *"The Hebrew women are not like the Egyptian women," the midwives replied. "They are more vigorous and have their babies so quickly that we cannot get there in time."* (NLT)

This could just have been a cover up on their part, but if it is, it comes out of their years of experience as midwives. Some women are delicate in labour, but some are vigorous and give birth quickly. Now that's the kind of pregnant woman I want to be!

This is a possibility. Whatever bumps may lie ahead, God wants the best for you. I made a decision that I would pursue God's best for my pregnancies, just like I had desired God's best for every area of my life. I handed over my pregnancies to Him and politely shut out people's horror stories of how they survived their pregnancy and labour. That was their story, but I wanted to be able to work out my journey with God, without having other people's tales going around in my head. I encourage you to do the same.

After much reflection I could think of no better starting point than to study God's Word and see what He had to say about my unborn child to help prepare me for the months ahead. This journey showed me that God is not only interested in my labour, but in my unborn child.

My first pregnancy

I knew from the morning after Joshua was conceived that I was pregnant. Everything felt different. My feelings were confirmed when one day at work, as I was working at my computer, I felt an incredible urge to throw up, totally out of the blue, then felt perfectly fine afterwards. A few of my workmates suggested that I must be pregnant, but I brushed it off as I hadn't yet taken a test.

That weekend my husband and I were going away to a leaders retreat from our church. Halfway through the weekend my stomach bloated to twice its size and it steadily grew bigger. We were concerned because of the rate at which my stomach was growing and went to the local hospital for a check-up.

On arrival, the nurse took a pregnancy test and confirmed we were pregnant. While we were overjoyed with this news, we were still concerned as to why my stomach was like this. The doctors thought it might be an ectopic pregnancy, but when further tests were made they came back fine, much to our relief. I still don't know why my body reacted like that, but it caused us to prioritise our prayers for our unborn child.

As the months went by, I soaked myself in God's Word for my child and even stopped people politely in their tracks if they tried to recount the horror stories of their pregnancies. I believed that I would be able to use my story to give God glory.

Two weeks before Joshua was due, I finished work. I didn't want to stay at home and do nothing, so I joined my husband in the church office to help him prepare for a family conference that was coming up, keeping my maternity bag in the car, just in case.

Then one morning Olly said that I looked tired and suggested I should stay in bed to rest. I put up a little fight, but after he went to work I fell into a deep sleep until lunch. After lunch I went to the office to help out again. The family conference was the next day, so we had lots of loose ends that needed to be completed.

Early in the evening we were still in the office when my first contraction started. I ignored it, thinking I had lots of time, but quite quickly the contractions started to intensify, so I went for a walk around the building to find my husband. He was in the middle of a conversation with a colleague and I wanted Olly to be the first to know what was going on, so I stood and controlled my facial expressions until I could tell him.

Olly asked me if I thought we had time to drop off everything at the church building, so that everything would be ready for the team to use the next day. As it was my first labour I thought we would have plenty of time. The journey to the church was an interesting one as the contractions became more intense.

Olly ran into the church and dropped off all the boxes and we then set off for the hospital, phoning them en route. The midwife stated that if I could talk through my contractions then I should wait a little longer. As she was speaking the most amazing contraction came and I knew we needed to be in the hospital. We arrived, checked into our room and after only 4 hours and 20 minutes of labour, using just four puffs of gas and air, our special little boy Joshua was born. We didn't make it to the church's family conference, but had our own personal family conference in the hospital. God was so good!

God took me on a journey during my first pregnancy. I learnt to trust Him with all the details. He was my heavenly Father, looking after His daughter, teaching me new things about Him and His love for me and my unborn child.

Woman, you are amazing

> "Oh yes, you shaped me first inside, then out;
> You formed me in my mother's womb.
> I thank You, High God—You're breath-taking!
> Body and soul, I am marvellously made!
> I worship in adoration—what a creation!
> You know me inside and out,
> You know every bone in my body;
> You know exactly how I was made, bit by bit,
> how I was sculpted from nothing into something.
> Like an open book, You watched me grow from conception to birth;
> all the stages of my life were spread out before You.
> The days of my life all prepared before I'd even lived one day.
>
> Psalm 139:13–16 (MSG)

Just in case you didn't know: *woman, you are amazing!* Your body is a living miracle, made by God to be able to get through what most men wouldn't even like to try to imagine.

It begins from the moment we conceive. Almost immediately, a woman's body begins to change. You may feel something is different right from day one after conception, as a series of changes is triggered. In life, a woman's body will rarely experience the number of rapid and dramatic changes as it does during pregnancy—but that is the way God has made you and it is all part of preparing you for the birth of your beautiful baby.

Many women see the second trimester as the easiest of the three, as their energy begins to return and, for most people, the sickness subsides. I certainly felt the difference as my body settled down into pregnancy into the second trimester. God has also created our bodies in such a way that our ligaments, tendons and cartilage soften and relax during pregnancy, in preparation for that wonderful time of labour, so that our baby can make its way past the pelvis.

The pregnant body has a number of such tricks up its sleeve. The appropriately named hormone relaxin affects the cartilage holding our bones together, so that it relaxes, making labour a lot easier. It isn't just targeted to the pelvis, however, but also to other parts of our body. Relaxin is present at 10 times its normal levels during pregnancy and affects all the joints in the body. It is one reason why some women experience some joint and back pain as their pregnancy progresses. Some women even increase a shoe size because of it.

God has also made it so that our bodies create 50% more blood during pregnancy. All the hard work of pregnancy requires more blood vessels and more blood. By the 20th week of pregnancy, our body may have up to 50% more blood than it did when we conceived. This is why many women glow when they are pregnant and look so well, with a radiant complexion. This additional blood helps with the extra flow of nutrients to the baby.

Isn't God amazing? He placed the right hormones inside us and even a completely new, temporary body part called the placenta, which changes the way our muscles work, allowing our baby to receive food and oxygen from us, even though they have not yet experienced the outside world. God gives us the ability to feed and nurture our child, all before they are born!

When it comes to the birth He has it all planned too. The bones of the baby's head are designed to be soft and have the ability to move slightly, so that they can gently mould to their mother's shape.

If a mother is giving birth in a more upright position, her sacrum (tail bone) can gently hinge itself to move out of the baby's way, providing 30% more space in the pelvis than normal to ease the baby's passage.

If a mother is not in an appropriate or safe place to give birth, her body will often stall the labour for a little while, to give her time to get to a safe place. This can happen, for instance, during the time it takes for a woman to get from home to the hospital. It then takes a little time for her to relax into the hospital setting and for the labour to get going again.

The birth hormone, *oxytocin*, causes a mother to process her labour using the back of her brain, which is not so complex. She can feel deeply relaxed or far away and will receive many less pain signals. A mother's pain threshold even increases naturally from 37 weeks of pregnancy.

God has planned for women to nurture, labour and give birth to children. He is completely and utterly in charge of your baby's growth! Being pregnant is a miracle.

> *The womb is the workshop of God*
> *You made all the delicate, inner parts of my body*
> *and knit me together in my mother's womb.*
> *Thank you for making me so wonderfully complex!*
> *Your workmanship is marvellous—how well I know it.*
> *You watched me as I was being formed in utter seclusion,*
> *as I was woven together in the dark of the womb.*
> *You saw me before I was born.*
> *Every day of my life was recorded in Your book.*
> *Every moment was laid out before a single day had passed.*
>
> Psalm 139:13–16

God, our Creator, has the best knitting pattern in the world—you and me! He made every part of us for a specific reason—from the tiny bones in our ears that pick up vibration and interpret sound waves, to the way in which our bodies react to various changes around us, such as temperature. God made it so that a woman's body instinctively knows what to do while it is preparing to give birth to a baby. God is amazing! The very fact that another human being can grow in our bodies from the tiniest cells is astonishing in itself, and makes us wonder all the more at God's creation.

Going to my first ever baby scan and seeing my son's heart pumping and him wiggling and squirming inside of me, made me marvel at God's creation. He started from a single cell and now God was growing him into the most amazing baby... inside of me! I still look back and wonder at that intimate time of God doing such a wonderful thing inside my body.

The wonder of conception, pregnancy and birth show the extraordinarily personal way in which God is involved in each of our lives. He worked to form us inside our mother's womb. He decided what we would look like, how tall we would be, whether we would have thin or thick hair, counting those hairs one by one, He knew our thoughts and also our destiny as He created us. This is true of every baby in any mother's womb—your child is immeasurably special to God. He delights in what He has created and He knew everything about your child's life even before conception.

Practical preparation

God is ultimately in control of our labour and the birth of our babies. He is the One who is working in us, creating new life. Yet, at the same time, He chooses to partner with us. We can plan to be a vigorous woman in birth and as much as possible help prepare our bodies for labour.

David was called to be a king and anointed as king as a young man, but he still had to go through a period of preparation. He worked as a shepherd and took decisions about how he was going to spend his time on earth. Every man or woman in the Bible who lived for God had to choose to play their part. They had to decide to cooperate with God's best for their life.

Proverbs 31 describes the "good wife" as one who strengthens herself, saying:

> *"She girds herself with strength [spiritual, mental, and physical fitness for her God-given task] and makes her arms strong and firm."*
>
> Proverbs 31:7 AMP

What might this look like for the pregnant woman? Here are some practical pointers:

Be active. Take the time to do your pelvic floor muscle exercises. If necessary, give yourself a daily reminder. Linking exercising your pelvic floor to some everyday action that you perform. If you regularly go to the photocopier, use this time as a time to exercise those pelvic floors! Perhaps meal times would be a great time to do them.

Take advantage of the middle months, when many women feel strong, not sick and not too tired. Use this time to build up your stamina and fitness. Exercise regularly and prepare your body, so that you can be a vigorous woman. Lying on the sofa all day will not help you to strengthen your body. In some pregnancies this may be all you are permitted or able to do. However, if you are feeling well and there is no danger to the baby, then we encourage you to get up and get moving. Be a vigorous woman.

> *"Good planning and hard work lead to prosperity, but hasty shortcuts lead to poverty."*
>
> Proverbs 21:15

Be healthy. Eat well. By all means enjoy treats, but also treat yourself to healthy food during your pregnancy. Feed your body and your baby with the best, freshest food you can find and enjoy the benefits of looking after your body.

> *"My child, don't lose sight of common sense and discernment. Hang on to them, for they will refresh your soul. They are like jewels on a necklace. They keep you safe on your way, and your feet will not stumble. You can go to bed without fear; you will lie down and sleep soundly."*
>
> Proverbs 3:13–21

Rest well. Sometimes sleep can be elusive, especially near the end of a pregnancy. At other times we are tired because we simply did not give ourselves enough time to rest. Be wise and give yourself the rest you need while you can. A rested woman is ready to be a vigorous woman.

> *"It is useless for you to work so hard from early morning until late at night, anxiously working for food to eat; for God gives rest to His loved ones."*
>
> Psalm 127:2

Be wise. You know what your body can do. You know what your body needs. Keep all your antenatal appointments and learn as much as you can about each stage of your pregnancy, so that you can make wise decisions which will benefit both you and your whole family. Decide to have a mind set that says you will be a vigorous woman. Even if you are flat on your back, unable to move, decide to be a vigorous woman! Don't be passive and fearful, but choose to partner with God and invest in your physical body.

> *"Wise choices will watch over you. Understanding will keep you safe."*
>
> Proverbs 2:11

Healthy, active women often have healthier, active labours. It's worth the effort.

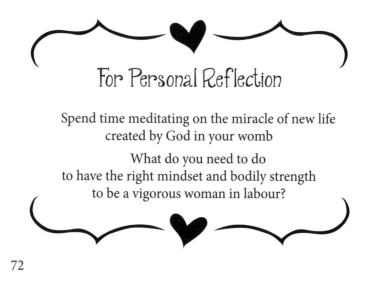

For Personal Reflection

Spend time meditating on the miracle of new life created by God in your womb

What do you need to do to have the right mindset and bodily strength to be a vigorous woman in labour?

9

You Have Your Own Story

"Lean on, trust in, and be confident in the Lord with all your heart and mind and do not rely on your own insight or understanding. In all your ways know, recognise, and acknowledge Him, and He will direct and make straight and plain your paths."

Proverbs 3:5–6 AMP

Each person's experience of pregnancy is different and we all respond to its challenges differently. Every person has a unique story about what God did for them during their pregnancy. As Christian women we are called to trust God throughout our lives, but often pregnancy is a time when we find ourselves leaning on Him more, as He creates new life inside us.

This fallen world

We live in a fallen world and we have an enemy, Satan, who is described as the prince of this world. Satan wants to destroy life and is not afraid to start his work in the womb.

When Moses, the leader of God's deliverance from Egyptian slavery and bringer of the Ten Commandments, was due to be born the enemy hatched a plot to exterminate all male infants. When Jesus, the bringer of salvation under the New Covenant, was born the enemy tried to destroy Him using the same tactic. Each time he failed to destroy those whom God had called to fulfil His purposes.

Yet he still tries the same tactic today. Thankfully, the Bible is clear and reassures us that God is more powerful than Satan by far. God sits on His throne and laughs at His enemies (Psalm 2:4). At the end of time it will take just one angel to throw Satan into hell (Revelation 20:1–3). When God rises up, His enemies have to flee (Psalm 68:1). More than that, He has given us His Holy Spirit to live within us:

"But you belong to God, my dear children. You have already won a victory over those people, because the Spirit who lives in you is greater than the spirit who lives in the world."

1 John 4:4

When things don't go according to plan

At the same time, we know that Satan is active from the moment life is conceived in the womb and still desires to steal, kill and destroy. In John 10:10 Jesus says, *"The thief's purpose is to steal and kill and destroy. My purpose is to give them a rich and satisfying life."*

As believers we are caught up in a war, a supernatural conflict that has implications for us, and at times we need to battle through, trusting in God's goodness despite adverse circumstances. Sometimes, pregnancies don't run as planned. So how can we deal with negative news concerning our baby?

For some, any bad news you receive will be something you know to fight against. For others it will be a journey to walk through with God. Either way, we must trust that God is in charge.

"Trust in the Lord with all your heart; do not depend on your own understanding. Seek His will in all you do, and He will show you which path to take."

Proverbs 3:5–6

Aidan's story—disaster looms

"Six years ago I was pregnant with my third child. Both my previous pregnancies had been different to each other, but nothing more troublesome than the normal things pregnant women go through.

"Aidan's story begins before I became pregnant. I knew God wanted us to have a third child, even though I really wasn't very keen on the idea. Morning sickness is just not my thing! I knew the baby would be a boy and we were to call him Aidan (after the Celtic evangelist St Aidan).

"I spent my days looking after Annabelle, who was the most adorable toddler and getting ready for Christmas. Melissa was at school and I was getting into that routine too! I started to feel better just before Christmas and was so relieved to be able to appreciate food again in time for our Christmas dinner!

"My scan was due at the start of January. Annabelle's second birthday was on the fifth of January, so I was busy thinking about her party as well as the start of a new term. I really didn't think much about my scan—it was just one of those things you do. But really, I wish I had been able to pray and prepare myself beforehand. Maybe then I would not have been caught so 'off guard'.

"The enemy of our souls is like a thief in the night who comes to kill and destroy . I found out the hard way that day.

"The day of my 20-week scan arrived. The lady in the scanning room was somewhat evasive and too cautious for my liking. She said she had to leave for a moment and scuttled off. I just knew something was terribly wrong. Thoughts were racing through my mind. I thought of our close friends who had recently seen their child die due to a horrid genetic syndrome. It was not something I would wish on anyone, let alone expect for this baby in my womb. Was the same thing about to happen to us?

"It seemed like time had stopped as we waited for the lady to return. A different woman came into the room armed with a clipboard (that's the only thing I can remember about her). She was very efficient and abrupt. 'I am from the High Risk Team,' she explained.

"My brain scrambled at this point. '"High risk"? Isn't that what bungee jumping is?' I wanted to say. 'Well that's okay then, because I'm not planning on surfing, scuba diving or bungee jumping right now, so you are in THE WRONG ROOM!'

"I soon found out that 'high risk' means there is something potentially wrong with your baby and she was there to tell me that, in her ever so matter-of-fact fashion. They say 'don't shoot the messenger,' but I really wanted to kill someone at that precise moment. I also wanted to faint with fear as it wrapped itself around my throat.

"The High Risk lady explained: 'The scan has shown us that your baby has two soft markers on its head and these are indications of a syndrome being present. This syndrome is called Edward's Syndrome.'

"We wondered what all her words meant. I remember looking at my husband for some kind of insight into this new jargon. She went on to explain what this meant for the baby and for me and for our family.

"You may wonder what we did in response to this news. We looked at each other and burst out laughing. It really wasn't a laughing matter, but human emotion is confusing and we were confused. They explained that our baby had a very high chance of being very poorly and could possibly die.

"The penny suddenly dropped. We knew all about Edward's Syndrome. This was what our friends had been through. I couldn't believe that this could happen all over again. Surely not? How could I carry a child that was only going to die? I was sick to my stomach.

"The lady with the clipboard explained our options. 'It is advisable to abort a child with Edward's Syndrome,' she stated simply. This was too much to take in. We could have all sorts of further tests, she said, but these may put the baby at risk. We could also come back in a couple of weeks to have a 3D scan, that may give us a bit more of an idea of the condition of our baby. We agreed to have the scan and left the hospital in a daze.

"I didn't understand. 'God, how could you do this to us?' I asked. 'How can you give us life and then take it away? Why are you putting us through this?' I screamed inside.

"The next week was a complete nightmare. Every day I cried. I didn't sleep well. I shouted at God. I felt utter panic and shock. I still had to manage Annabelle's party. But how could I? People didn't know what I was going through. What could I say to them? How would I cope with the well-meaning comments about this pregnancy?

"Then God spoke to me very clearly one day and took me to Psalm 27, saying, 'This is a Psalm for the baby.' We now call it Aidan's Psalm and it's on the wall of his bedroom. One verse in particular stuck out:

*"Yet I am confident I will see the Lord's goodness while
I am here in the land of the living."*

Psalm 27:13

"God had spoken. I now had a choice. Which word was I going to believe?

"Every day I had to make that choice again. I was going to believe what God had said to me, instead of what the doctors were telling me.

"This did not mean that my feelings followed suit. They didn't. Some days I was good, other days were horrendous. We went for the scan and I was petrified. My husband was calm on the outside, but I knew it was hard for him too. The lady consultant was warm and reassuring. I waited in agony while she got the picture of our baby on the screen in front of me.

"It looked fine to me. I was waiting for her to give me the bad news, but she did not give me any news, she just explained my baby to me. She told me it had a beautiful face, all its fingers and toes. She was looking for further signs of Edward's syndrome. She asked if I wanted to know what sex it was. She wanted to tell me because Edward's Syndrome is more prevalent in boys.

"'You are having a boy. Let's look at his "bits",' she said. 'Oh yes, all fine there.' Later I learned that Edward's boys have undeveloped sexual organs and they have a curled up little finger. She was giving me clues as to my baby's health, but she did not say what I wanted to hear. I wanted her to tell us that my baby was okay. After the scan she explained to me that I could still go ahead and abort this child and that the chances of it having Edward's Syndrome were about 1 in 200.

"That seems huge now and I wonder what I was so fretful for, but back then it felt like a death sentence. We left the hospital. God had told us that, '*You will see the goodness of the Lord in the land of the living.*' We didn't abort him. Instead, we chose to complete the pregnancy and put it in God's hands.

"Aidan was born on 2 June 2003, a whopping 9 pounds 14 ounces, after a short labour of about 3 hours. He fed straight away and kept feeding every day after that. He did not have Edward's Syndrome. He had, and has, *life!*

"This is not a story of healing. He never had anything wrong with him. This is a story of how the enemy of our souls wants to kill us and our children. Aidan is the most amazing gift from God to us and to all who know him. His story has taught us many things. *He* has taught us many things. Our life is blessed because Aidan is in it and we are so glad that we went through with what God asked of us—to bring this child into the world.

"That was not the end of the story. After all the emotional trauma of the pregnancy I developed post-natal depression. These things affect us emotionally, but I am now completely recovered. We are putting it all behind us and enjoying the blessing that God has given us, and seeing His goodness in the land of the living."

Trust God

If you are given bad news about your pregnancy, the first step is to trust God. He is still in charge of you and your baby. Take the issue to God and ask Him to speak to you about what you should do. Is this something He wants to walk through with you or is this something in which He is calling you to trust Him for His plan?

Faith can be defined as believing what God says more than what we see with our eyes. God's word has to be the starting point of such faith. God can and does heal people today. He is the one who is growing the babies in the womb. He can heal children in the womb.

All we want is life

One family we prayed with were told very clearly by their doctors to abort their child. They knew this was not God's plan.

The doctors started regular scans. "You know that your baby cannot live," they said. "They have no brain, no lungs, no heartbeat. You will be giving birth to a stillborn child."

Yet the parents had a word from God that there would be breath in their child's lungs. As we prayed with them they kept saying, we are not believing God for perfect health. We just want this baby to have life. Every time we pray we keep hearing that God wants this child to live.

The doctors continued the weekly scans. Still there was no brain, no lungs, no heartbeat. They were concerned for this couple who did not seem to be taking on board the fact that their baby had no life.

Then the scan at 38 weeks showed the flicker of a heartbeat. Life. The first sign of life.

The doctors cautioned against this good news: "There is still no brain and no lungs. This foetus is not viable."

But the parents had their word from God and this was their first flicker of an answer. At 39 weeks the report was the same. The doctors discussed inducing the labour. The parents had received a word from God in prayer and were waiting to see how this no brain, no lung baby would turn out. They wanted to wait until the baby was officially overdue before making any decisions.

At 40 weeks, exactly on the due date, their baby was born. As soon as he came out of the womb he started to breathe spontaneously. God had given the child life. He still had some significant health problems, but he was here. He was breathing. He was alive.

Many families have had to walk through such trials. For my sixth pregnancy we had the challenge of hearing continually bad news from the doctors.

You are diabetic

During the week we conceived baby 'Godly Example', for the first time in any of my pregnancies, I had the urge to have a girl. It lasted for about a week. Before then we had never tried for a girl, just a baby, but at that point God gave me the longing to have a girl.

By this point I was officially *old*. That happens on your 40th birthday, according to the doctors in our hospital. I was offered checks to see if my baby had Down's Syndrome, which I declined. I knew that God had a destiny for my child, no matter what, and that we wanted them, however God had ordained for them to be.

I went for my blood sugar test and was told I had high sugar levels. I was duly given the label 'gestational diabetic'. With this, I knew my faith levels needed to rise. I was told in no uncertain terms that I would not be allowed a birth centre birth, which I had enjoyed for my previous four labours, now I would have to go into the medical ward for delivery.

This was the start of all God's miracles. We went for our 20-week scan and, for the first time, we discovered the sex of our child. We were having a girl! Until that point I didn't think I had the right ingredients to produce girls (my four boys seemed proof enough of that), but God had heard my desire, albeit short lived, to have a girl. God was in control.

I had to go regularly to the diabetic clinic in the hospital to have my bloods checked and meet with the consultant. Each time I met with the consultant I would tell him how well I was feeling, how my bloods were coming back normal after every meal and that my baby would be fine. He told me that there could still be complications with the baby, but my faith stayed with God that there would be no complications with this pregnancy. I just knew, my body knew and God knew. Each time we met, he told me what should be happening to someone with my condition and each time I showed him that that wasn't happening to me. At every scan my baby was an average weight for that stage of the pregnancy and the placenta fluid remained at a normal volume. Nevertheless, I was still being told that I could not have a 'non-medicalised' birth, since the risk was too great.

As I approached my 39th week of pregnancy my consultant was suggesting that I should be induced, but I couldn't see why this was necessary. My baby was an average size for the date, my bloods were okay, and I felt well. I told the hospital midwives that if the doctors had discovered a risk to my baby then I would go ahead, but if not I wanted God's timing for my baby's birth.

The midwives had obviously fed back my thoughts to the consultant prior to our next meeting and he walked in with a smile. "You can have your way, this baby will not be induced," he told me. The midwifery staff later told me with a chuckle that no one normally got their own way with that particular consultant. God came through as we prayed into the situation.

Although the baby wouldn't be induced, I still had to have a medical birth, so I decided to go and visit the ward, so I would know where I'd be going in due course. In the ward there was a room that had a birthing pool, which was just like the birthing centre, and I claimed that for me for when I went in.

I went in for my 40-week check. On this occasion I felt God say that I should go by public transport rather than by car. My consultant handed me over to a female registrar who wanted to give me a sweep to start me off. I explained that I had come by train and I wouldn't want to risk going back on the train as my labours have all been so quick. At that point, she also told me that I could have a water birth, which was the first time I had been told that formally.

I went home and told Olly that the doctors wanted me to go back to hospital a week later for a sweep and they wanted to strap monitors on me from the moment I arrived to check the baby's heart rate. This was something which I only wanted to do if other indicators showed it to be necessary. I believed God for 'Godly Example' to arrive before that appointment. God had been involved in every detail of this pregnancy. I was grateful to God for the diligent work of the doctors and midwives, who were ready to give me all the support modern medicine has to offer, if needed. But God had given me faith to believe that none of this help would be required for this child.

That weekend I went into labour. We called the labour ward to let them know we were coming and asked if the room with the birthing pool was available. God had kept it free for me and they started to fill the tank.

On arrival they asked me to wait in reception. No one was rushing because I was so calm and we waited for 10 minutes. A lovely midwife came to me. I was taken to the room whilst she read my notes and realised I was supposed to be hooked up to a monitor continuously. Even in this God was going have the last laugh. She went out to get the monitor and brought it back. It wouldn't work. I giggled, realising that God was answering all my prayers. She left the room to fetch another monitor, but during that time my waters broke. Three pushes later beautiful Abigail was born.

I had been in labour for 1 hour and 20 minutes. The labour was too quick for them to completely fill the birthing pool, but quick enough for God to answer my prayers for a non-medicalised birth. God is so faithful. I know that I have been blessed with my labours, but put God in charge and He will organise all your heart's desires to happen in the labour room experience!

Through prayer babies have turned around in the womb to face head down before labour, beaten the odds to be born without abnormalities and been born a normal weight against doctors' expectations. In short, God has done many miracles in the womb. The greatest miracle of all is that He is the Giver of life.

My fourth pregnancy had proven to be more of a challenge than this.

Between pregnancies three and four I had suffered a ruptured appendix, which had stuck to my fallopian tube. Around 6 months after this I became pregnant with my fourth child. We gave this child the name 'Abundant Joy'. As with all our other children, I spoke and prayed with Abundant Joy and grew to love them within the womb. When we were around 9 weeks pregnant, coming up to our first scan, when I went to the toilet and saw blood. My heart sank. We made our way to the hospital.

They took a scan, but because I was so early they said a scan wouldn't show what was going on, even though they could see that my womb was there. They asked me to come back the next day for a further check, at which point they found that baby Abundant Joy was no longer there. Tears came, but I knew that God was in control.

It is hard to know why these things happen, but I know I will meet Abundant Joy in heaven. We told our children that their sibling was now with Jesus. They took it on board and still refer to Abundant Joy as the baby that Jesus wanted to keep.

If this has happened to you, you may not understand why things have turned out as they have, and your emotions will be pulling you all over the place. But trust that God remains sovereign over it all. He has a plan, even though you may not see what it is yet.

If you are in the midst of a difficult pregnancy, remember that God is still at the centre of it. This does not mean we should ignore the advice of medical practitioners, though some of what they say may be hard to hear. It may go against your hopes for your baby or it may feed your worst fears, but listen to God. For some, God will give you a clear word from Him to combat the negative words you have heard. For others, it may be that the doctors are the very agents God will use to deliver your baby safely.

Faith trusts that God is in charge, however things turn out. God works both through those around us as well as by His Spirit.

Ask God to give you a word. An assurance from God is something to hold on to in turbulent times. If you are finding it hard to hear from God in the midst of the storm, ask others to pray for you.

When you have the word from God write it down and stick it up on your wall. Pray it in your heart and hold on to it for the journey ahead. There is no news you can hear that will take God by surprise. There is no problem too great that He cannot carry you through it.

God is good.

The child with special needs

If this section is not relevant to you, feel free to skip this bit and jump ahead to the next section where we look at how we can help prepare the whole family for the new addition that God is blessing you with.

If God gives you a child with special needs it is not the end of the world. Instead, it is the start of a journey. God has a plan for each child and every one is special to Him. It may be that you have feelings of anger, confusion or of being let down by God—it can be hard to see God's eternal plan for us and our children—but this doesn't alter the fact of His goodness and His commitment to give each of His children the very best. Many have discovered reports of syndromes in the womb to be unfounded when the baby is born. Others have simply discovered God in a more profound way in the midst of their trials.

I share with you this poem that has helped many women who have walked this journey before you.

Heaven's Very Special Child

A meeting was held quite far from Earth!
It's time again for another birth.
Said the Angels to the Lord above,
This Special Child will need much love.

His progress may be very slow,
Accomplishments he may not show.
And he'll require extra care
From the folks he meets down there.

He may not run or laugh or play,
His thoughts may seem quite far away,
In many ways he won't adapt,
And he'll be known as handicapped.

So let's be careful where he's sent,
We want his life to be content.
Please Lord, find the parents who
Will do a special job for you.

They will not realise right away,
The leading role they're asked to play,
But with this child sent from above,
Comes stronger faith and richer love.

And soon they'll know the privilege given
In caring for their gift from Heaven.
Their precious charge, so meek and mild,
Is HEAVEN'S VERY SPECIAL CHILD.

Edna Massionilla, December 1981[3]

It takes a very special kind of person to see and take joy in the life of their child with special needs. As parents travel this journey, God gives some a faith to see their child's health improve and to others He gives strength to walk the journey. These special children bring great joy alongside the heartache. In different ways we all have special needs of various degrees and God the Father continues to use us as He wants to. These children will become a precious part of your family and often enrich the lives of those around them far more than anyone could expect.

---

[3] From *The Optimist* newsletter for PROUD—Parents Regional Outreach for Understanding Downs Inc.

In the meantime don't be harsh on yourself. Many parents of children with special needs find themselves grieving the loss of health of their child. If those feelings are not dealt with, then can turn inwards, and the parents can feel guilty as they look at the child God has blessed them with. Take one day at a time and allow yourselves to trust that God is over it all.

Nick Vujicic was born with a rare disorder shown by the absence of all four limbs. As a child, he struggled mentally and emotionally as well as physically, but eventually came to terms with his disability. At the age of seventeen he started his own non-profit organisation, Life Without Limbs. Nick now presents motivational speeches worldwide on life with a disability, hope, and finding meaning in life. He also speaks about his belief that God can use any willing heart to do His work and that God is big enough to overcome any and all disabilities.[4]

This man lives life to the full and brings encouragement and hope to those around him. He breaks down the barriers of misconception and shows what God can do through one person who trusts in Him. Nick is an example of someone who has many extra needs, yet God has made him an overcomer and marked out a plan for His life as He will for your child too! Ask God for that word for your child to hold on to in the times ahead.

❤❤❤❤❤

In this section we have seen the value of the unborn child. We have learnt how we can minister to our child whilst they are still in the womb. Time will go quickly. Before long they will arrive in the world. Then you will be holding in your hands a powerful instrument for God to use.

In the next section we will be discussing how we can prepare our whole family to welcome this new baby.

---

[4] Taken from Wikipedia

For Personal Reflection

Do you trust that God knows
what is best for your family?

Part 2
Preparing as a Family

10

Families are God's Idea

The centre of society

Family is God's idea. From the start God saw that Adam needed human company to enjoy life to the full. God said in Genesis 2:18, *"It is not good for the man to be alone. I will make a helper who is just right for him."* So Eve was created to help Adam. Then, His plan was that people would eventually leave the family units they were raised in, to create new family units of parents and children (Genesis 2:24).

When God sees someone who needs people around them, He does not send them to a social centre or to the government. He does not even send them to their neighbours or the local church. Instead, *"God places the lonely in families,"* says Psalm 68:6. This statement gives us an insight into the intimate relationships that God desires all people to enjoy and be a part of.

The way we relate to each other in our families matters to God. He wants our hearts to be for the other members of our family. Indeed, the very last verse of the Old Testament speaks about families being restored or else the whole land will be cursed:

> *"His preaching will turn the hearts of fathers to their children, and the hearts of children to their fathers. Otherwise I will come and strike the land with a curse."*
>
> Malachi 4:6

The family is at the very centre of society. From within the family children gain their sense of security and self-worth. Many issues that people try to deal with in adulthood via counselling can be traced back to unresolved childhood issues. For a strong society to develop, families need not just to live together, but to be stable, happy places. This is a well established, thoroughly researched fact.

Families are the primary context in which God chooses for children to be raised and to learn about Him. Deuteronomy 6:7 points us in this direction. The Jewish family model bears testament to how effective family based, community learning can be. A fuller discussion on this topic can be found in our book on parenting.

Children are our joy and privilege. Psalm 127 describes children as an inheritance from the Lord. Proverbs 17:6 says, *"Grandchildren are the crowning glory of the aged; parents are the pride of their children."* Many older people speak with joy about their family. The continuance of the family line adds great value to the end of a person's life as they see the legacy they are leaving behind. When deciding between children and work, very few people lie on their death beds thinking, "I wish I'd spent more time at work."

So families are a priority for God and we should make our family our priority. This will require some juggling on our part. Whatever your family was like growing up, determine to learn from the good and the bad to provide the best environment you can for your children.

The perfect family

The perfect family does not exist! Families are made up of imperfect people and they bring these imperfections into the family. Imperfect families are the norm. Husbands and wives can argue, siblings can squabble, and families can be broken apart. For some women, the father of their child may not be around anymore. Broken families are part of living in a fallen world.

This does not change the fact that the creation of families was God's idea. God has not created a Plan B to replace the family. The family is God's only plan. Whatever challenges you face in your family, be they trivial or seemingly insurmountable, God sees the family unit as good and fit for purpose. Problems in families are nothing new and God is for all people in all types of families. Broken families have been around since the time when Adam and Eve had Cain and Abel.

The Bible deals with the reality of modern families. If you are in any doubt about God's love for imperfect families, take a look at the families of three of the most highly respected people in the Bible: The patriarchs—Abraham, Isaac and Jacob.

Abraham fathered Ishmael and showed him great love at the start (Genesis 21:11). He also had other children through other women (Genesis 25:1–4). He then rejected all his children except Isaac, sending them away (Genesis 25:5–6). Before Isaac was born, Sarah had to cope with infertility and jealousy from her servant.

Isaac and Rebekah did not see eye-to-eye on every issue.

Take a look at how Sarah encouraged Jacob to trick his own father, her husband, into giving his blessing. There was clearly marital disagreements in this family.

Jacob and Esau had one of the worst cases of sibling rivalry recorded. Jacob, the deceiver, tricked his brother. Esau wanted to kill Jacob.

As for Jacob, his family was as complex as any modern family. There were half-brothers, wives (loved and unloved), mistresses, sibling rivalry in the extreme, parental favouritism and division at every level.

This is not to mention Tamar, whose own family called her a prostitute, even though she had been more honourable than her accusers! (Genesis 38:14–26)

Biblical families were not so different from our modern families. We see messed up families throughout Scripture. Consider Eli, the weak father. Think about Samuel, who did not grow up with a good model of family to follow and was so busy with his job that his children went astray.

No matter what your personal family backgrounds are like, decide together as husband and wife that your family will break this cycle. Ask God for His mercy to make your family a turning point for the better.

If the family you grew up in was happy and stable, copy all that was good. If you consider your family to have had weaknesses or even to have been completely broken, decide that your generation will be the one to change this pattern. You cannot bring up your child in isolation from a family, even if the family only consists of the two of you. After all, broken families lead to hurting people who cause families to be broken even worse, leading to even more hurting people. As Hosea prophesies in chapter 8 verse 7, *"They sow the wind, and reap the whirlwind."*

When you consider your family, trust that God knows your situation and accepts you unconditionally. Also look to see what you can do to change things.

As Reinhold Niebuhr prayed:

> *God, grant me the serenity to accept the things I cannot change,*
> *The courage to change the things I can,*
> *And the wisdom to know the difference.*

Statistically, marriage between a man and a woman is best for the couple and for the children. Of course, statistics don't spell out the case for every individual. There are married couples whose children do less well than children from single parent families and children from single parent families who thrive throughout life. If you are part of a single parent family, God also promises to fill in the gaps. He promises in Psalm 68:5 that He is a father to the fatherless. God will take special care to watch over your family.

In nearly every family there are more people involved than mother and baby. For a season the baby will be the centre of attention in the family and the mother will be the gateway to the baby. This can affect every member of the family as each person tries to find their place in the new family.

The role of the mother and baby is clear in the first few weeks and months. Fathers, husbands and siblings may be less clear about what is expected of them and where they fit in. In the following chapters we will be exploring these different relationships to see how the whole family can prepare spiritually for the new baby.

Some of the following chapters may not be relevant for you in your family situation. For example, if your child's father is not around, or if this is your first child so there are no siblings to consider. If that's the case, feel free to skip to the next relevant chapter.

For Personal Reflection

Together with your partner,
reflect on your upbringings

What would you want to copy?

What would you want to do differently?

11

Building Your Marriage in Pregnancy

"I will make you my wife forever, showing you righteousness and justice, unfailing love and compassion."

Hosea 2:19

Precious time

What an adventure! Your baby is snug in the womb, your husband is by your side and all is calm. This is the perfect time to enjoy your marriage and make the most of that precious time as a couple without children. Of course, when your baby arrives that is precious too, but it will be different.

Having a child is a greater transition than getting married. Suddenly there is another, quite different factor in the equation that needs to be juggled. It is important, therefore, to make the most of your time together before your baby arrives. Building your marriage during this time will provide your little one with a strong, nurturing environment to come into.

When I married my husband one of the things we decided to do was set aside one night a week to be together. This was our 'date night'. All appointments were cancelled and nothing could get in the way of that night, except by mutual agreement. Protecting your time together is so important, especially when you have children. Life gets so busy that it is easy to make excuses as to why you are too busy or too tired to have a date.

Dedicated time together is very important to build into your marriage. Sometimes when we have our date nights we decide to avoid talking about the children, our work or the ministry. These three aspects of our lives are very important, but our marriage is more than the sum of these three things. In the busyness of the day we find time to communicate something on all these important topics, but when we are enjoying dedicated time together we want to make sure other things don't crowd in. To maintain a healthy marriage it is important to keep your mutual interests alive as you spend that valuable time together.

God created marriages to be spiritually strong. If your mutual relationship with God was strong as a married couple before your baby arrived, it will be easier to keep that going afterwards. The old saying, *families that pray together, stay together* is very true. Your partner is your teammate for life. Maintaining that close bond will provide a strong, united environment in which your children can thrive.

Now is the right time to conduct a marriage health check. Hairline fractures can become gaping chasms when a baby arrives. Newborn babies need attention and sleep deprivation can be a big problem. Tiredness brings out the worst in most of us, so teamwork is essential.

Children are smart. As they grow, they soon learn which parent is more likely to say yes to what request. They know how much mischief they can get away with. When we show a united front as parents, this helps our children understand their boundaries. It also helps us!

In marriage, two people become one. If you are fighting with your spouse you are fighting against yourself. In marriage, no one 'wins' an argument. One person may win a debate, but both people lose because of the temporary breakdown in communication and the expression of love. Most of the time, it is the small issues the are left unresolved that cause friction in a marriage. Find ways to resolve these issues before you drive each other crazy.

One couple chose to perform a monthly marriage health check together. At that time they would pray together, share things that they had been finding difficult within the marriage, pray again and then choose to discuss it no further. Out of love for each other they would then work on anything they could do to improve the marriage, based on what their spouse had said. This kind of regular health check will prevent problems from feeling insurmountable.

Sow into your marriage

Here are some ideas for keeping your marriage strong. Discuss them together and decide how you might want to adjust your lifestyles before the baby comes, to build some of these things into your weekly routine.

Pray together regularly. Prayer is such a key foundation to marriage. When we pray with someone it is hard to remain annoyed with them for long. If we manage to remain annoyed, God is quite good at pointing out our errors as you pray together!

Pray together for your baby, your marriage, your dreams and aspirations, and your respective callings. Pray for situations within your family life. Take authority over negative aspects in your family, marriage and children, submitting these issues to God. Pray blessings over each other and your whole family.

Have a date each week. This can be done in all kinds of ways. You may want to get dressed up and go out for a meal. If money is short, go for a romantic walk or just for a coffee together. Why not get the candles out, prepare a special meal and have a romantic night in? Leave little notes of love for one another and do things "just because" for no particular reason other than to express our love and appreciation. All this helps to make each partner in the marriage special.

Talk about your spouse behind their back... in a positive way! Forget the negative stuff, that's for the two of you to discuss on your own. Let others hear the good things you see in your partner. This will likely be fed back to them and it will also keep you focused on the positives in your spouse. Both these things will serve to build your marriage.

Instead of saying, "he's hopeless at changing nappies" try "he lets me sleep in when I've had a busy night" or "the other day he loaded the dishwasher for me."

Enjoy sexual intimacy together. The apostle Paul tells us not to withhold ourselves from each other without mutual agreement and then only for a time. It's not helpful. The act of sexual union brings union to a marriage on many levels. Of course, it may be a while after the baby is born before you feel ready for intercourse, but discuss this with your husband and don't leave him trying to guess what you are thinking.

Discuss your expectations for when the baby arrives. Who will do what? How will life be different? Prepare together and ask

God to come into the preparations to avoid unnecessary stress between you both. You cannot cover all aspects and things you agree may need to change once the reality of life with your baby comes, but starting the discussion before your baby is born will help to continue it once they arrive.

Encourage one another daily. Find something each day to encourage your spouse with. For instance, tell them that you know they will be the best mum or dad; say how much fun they are to be around; tell them they are a fantastic cook; tell them they are looking handsome or beautiful today. Look at your partner: there is so much you can encourage them about. The more you show them that you are for them, the better they will feel within your marriage and the easier it will be to negotiate any challenges that come your way as a family.

Don't forget to have fun together. Giggle together, laugh together, enjoy life together! With a child in the family life speeds up, don't let it pass you by.

Hold hands regularly… when you are walking together or sitting together. The joy of belonging together, to each other, will only add to your marriage. Enjoy each other's company.

If your marriage is facing difficulties that you cannot resolve, don't bury those difficulties under the business of preparing for a baby. Instead, seek godly counselling together.

For Personal Reflection

What state is your marriage in?
Choose two things that you can do
to strengthen your marriage

12

From Man to Dad

Men are an important part of child rearing, so here is a chapter especially for fathers-to-be. When my first child was born I looked at him and thought, "I want to be a hero to him." Of course, there is no greater privilege than others desiring to imitate you, but would I be able to live up to this standard?

In a time when the role of fathers is being constantly eroded by society, it is our immense privilege as Christians to understand that, with God's help, we can be a father to our children, even before they are born. In fact, our role as father to our children is arguably the most important role we'll play in our entire lives.

As with any privilege comes great responsibility. In this chapter we are going to explore how different men responded to this responsibility and had to adjust the way they lived in the light of it. May our enthusiasm for the Lord inspire our children and those around us to serve Him wholeheartedly.

> *"Love each other with genuine affection, and take delight in honouring each other. Never be lazy, but work hard and serve the Lord enthusiastically."*
>
> Romans 12:10–11

Ken—concerned for provision

"When my wife was pregnant with our first child I was so concerned with how I would provide for my growing family. I would need money for this, money for that… I was so worried about our finances. Really, I was just trying to do things in my own strength. That's what us guys do, after all, we want the best for our wife and child.

"Bright and early one morning I was out jogging, taking the same route as usual, but on this occasion it was different. The

Holy Spirit spoke to me in a gentle voice. 'Listen to those birds in that tree,' He said. I had passed this tree every time I'd been for a jog, but had never noticed the birds before. There were hundreds of them, singing beautifully. Then the Lord said to me: 'See those birds? They do not worry about what they are going to eat. I feed them. So you are not to worry either.'

"From that day onwards I had a peace about providing for my family and started focusing more on Jesus and what promises God has for my family and me. We now have three beautiful children and testimony after testimony of all that God has done in all our lives and in my business."

Justin—worried for the future

"When I found out my wife was pregnant a part of me was excited, but I was also very worried. When I was younger I had had a previous relationship. My partner had become pregnant, but the pregnancy was ectopic. Seeing my wife pregnant now brought out all kinds of emotions that I did not realise were still there.

"I went to a womb ministry session and prayed with other men. By half way through the pregnancy my fear was going and my excitement could at last take centre stage."

Don't worry, trust God

As the responsibility of fatherhood approaches, worry seems like a natural reaction: "Will I be a good father? Will my baby be healthy? How will this affect our marriage? How will I provide for my family? How will I balance my life?"

Underlying all these worries is the implication that we are responsible for everything. Yet we are not called to bear this responsibility alone. Instead, we need to give our worries to God and trust that He will give us solutions for all that lies ahead.

God is giving life to your child and He has worked out all the future details. Worrying will not help you, your wife or your child. Jesus spoke clearly about worry:

> *"That is why I tell you not to worry about everyday life—whether you have enough food and drink, or enough clothes to wear. Isn't life more than food, and*

your body more than clothing? Look at the birds.
They don't plant or harvest or store food in barns, for
your heavenly Father feeds them. And aren't you far
more valuable to Him than they are? Can all your
worries add a single moment to your life? And why
worry about your clothing? Look at the lilies of the
field and how they grow. They don't work or make
their clothing, yet Solomon in all his glory was not
dressed as beautifully as they are. And if God cares
so wonderfully for wildflowers that are here today
and thrown into the fire tomorrow, He will certainly
care for you. Why do you have so little faith? So don't
worry about these things, saying, 'What will we eat?
What will we drink? What will we wear?' These
things dominate the thoughts of unbelievers, but your
heavenly Father already knows all your needs. Seek
the Kingdom of God above all else, and live
righteously, and He will give you everything you need."

Matthew 6:25–33

God's solution to worry is to trust Him and seek His kingdom first of all. Make this your focus during the pregnancy—that your family will be part of the kingdom of God.

Don't back away, be involved

For some men, the looming responsibility of parenthood can cause them to withdraw. We hibernate in work, hobbies or friends. Yet this is the time when our wives need us more than ever, as her body is going through strange things it has never experienced before.

Decide to be actively involved and engaged in your baby's life while they are in the womb. Gone are the days when the men would avoid the labour room. In a world where the role of fathers is often undermined, we should delight in being involved with our babies as much as is practical while they are in the womb. Your wife will be grateful and you will enjoy being part of the miracle that is childbirth.

Here are some practical ways other men found they could be involved while their wives were pregnant.

Harley—supporting your wife

"It was such an amazing experience to have our baby growing in my wife's belly and to be able to place my hand on her ever expanding tummy and feel him in there.

"Morning sickness came like clockwork. Every day after work she would go into the toilet for a minute and then come out for her cut papaya (one of the things that she could eat and really enjoyed eating). There was always papaya in the fridge and I used to cut it up for her each day. She found it hard to eat normal foods at the start.

"There were lots of other practical things I found I could do to help her and build our marriage; from prayer to foot massages, from considering her feelings to helping her organise everything."

At different stages in life you are given more of an opportunity to die to self. This is one of those times. Take some photos, write a journal (if that is your thing), lay hands on the belly, and don't forget to enjoy this wonderful time.

Julian—spare ribs and worship

"I used to play the saxophone while Melissa worshiped. Melissa singing was the best way for our unborn child to hear worship music as it went direct from mother to baby. I've also got a great spare ribs recipe as my wife went nuts for spare ribs while she was pregnant!"

Jacqui—just what I needed

"My husband would put headphones on my tummy to play music to my babies. On hot days he would arrange a bowl of cool water to put my feet in. Add in lots of backrubs and 2.00 a.m. food runs to satisfy my cravings for slurpees and I felt so supported during our pregnancy."

Don't carry on as normal, prepare for change

Until you have children, no one can really tell you what it will be like. Not only is every person's experience different, but some things can only be truly understood through experience.

The one thing that we can say for certain is that things will be different. Let's celebrate the change that is coming and not pretend that everything will be the same.

Ben—time to change

"When my wife became pregnant I found myself talking to my wife's tummy about God and praying for the bump. I also had to watch my language when I was around my pregnant wife/baby."

Examine your life and see if there is anything that will have to change when you become a dad. It might be those long days at work or the clubs you go to regularly. It may be your attitude to your wife and family.

Tell your wife daily how beautiful she is. As she gets bigger, some women blossom in their pregnancy and know it. Others just feel bloated and fat. Your wife needs to know you still find her attractive during this time.

Encourage her to rest. Many mums don't realise how tired they have become. Pregnancy can be pretty exhausting. Giving her space to rest while you occupy the older children or help with the housework will do her and baby a world of good.

Now that your wife is pregnant is there anything she finds harder to do than before? Towards the end of pregnancy she may not find it so easy to carry the shopping, decorate the ceiling or even to put on her own shoes.

Don't abdicate your home responsibilities, lead the way

"But there is one thing I want you to know: The head of every man is Christ, the head of woman is man, and the head of Christ is God."

1 Corinthians 11:3

God has created man to be the head of the family unit.

For some, the mention of headship conjures up pictures of domineering, controlling men who make all the decisions; whose wives are like shadows in the background, there to serve the man's every need.

This is not the biblical definition of headship. Yes, Ephesians 5:22 makes it clear that wives are meant to submit to husbands and submission is really proved when someone submits against their own will and desires. This could imply that the woman is to obey her husband without thinking and without question. But it is only half the story. Verse 25 shows how husbands are to play their part in the marriage.

> *"For husbands, this means love your wives, just as Christ loved the church. He gave up His life for her."*
>
> Ephesians 5:25

The biblical picture of a husband is not someone barking out orders, but a man seeking the best for his wife and sacrificing his own desires for her sake. A man who truly loves his wife in this way will find that she has no trouble submitting to his lavish, generous, sacrificial leadership. Such leadership would want to hear his wife's view on all matters before making decisions. Such leadership would be willing to go against what he wants, so that his wife can be the best. Such leadership requires Christ.

Loving your wife through pregnancy and the early days of motherhood should be another expression of leadership. Take the lead when your wife is tired, to help her out. Take the lead spiritually to pray for your family. Love your wife as Christ loves the Church.

Pray and prophesy over your baby. Don't wait till your baby is born before you start spiritually nurturing them, start now while your baby is in the womb. Speak and declare God's words and promises over them.

Matt—labour interruptions

"I remember when both of my children were born. With my first child, I was nine miles into completing a ten mile sponsored walk when my father-in-law pulled up alongside us to say that my wife was in labour. I'm ashamed to say that my first thought was, 'Can I just finish the last mile?' You'll be pleased to know I did head off with my father-in-law, mainly due to the encouragement of others. Later that day, our wonderful son broke into the world.

"A few years later my wife woke me in the middle of the night to tell me she thought she was going into labour. Again, I'm ashamed to say that my first thought was, 'It's 3 o'clock in the morning!' But we got up and hours later our second son was born.

"Why do I share this? Because I'm learning more than anything, as a husband and father, the importance of being totally committed to serve and sacrifice my life for my wife and kids. The Bible tells us to love our wives as Christ loves the Church, and Jesus gives everything—His very life—for the Church.

"So my advice to every man reading this is to remember that your priority in life is to be good news to your wife and kids. To help them thrive. To put them first and make sure they know that they are first. They're more important than your ministry or your work or your friends. They are your first church and the primary outworking of your love for God.

"The love of Jesus gives to us without expecting anything in return. That's a massive challenge to our culture which promotes 'give and take'. But the good news is 'give and give'. Love your wife and kids whether they do nice stuff for you or not. That's the challenge. That's the call of Jesus. That's the kind of man I want to be. Selfless not selfish."

Ben's story—balance

"As we were preparing for our first child I was very anxious to know how I could balance my work with my family. I am self-employed in the media industry. Being self-employed I take work as it comes. Being in the media industry there are times when the deadlines can be tight and the hours long. I could not see how this was compatible with my desire to be with my family, so I sat with two colleagues in a similar line of work who were both fathers to see how they managed it.

"The first told me, 'Since I've had children my business has gone downhill. I cannot devote all the time that my business needs without being an absent father.' Not feeling very encouraged by this, I turned to my second friend. He told me, 'My business carries on as usual. Unfortunately, I don't get home until my child is in bed and I am usually out early in the morning. That's just the nature of this job.'

"I went away demoralised. How was I going to manage this impossible balance? I would have to depend on God."

Find balance and understand the seasons

This is a challenge most fathers have to face. There will not always be a right or a wrong answer, but it is helpful to think in terms of seasons. There will be seasons where we need to work harder and seasons where we can spend more time with the family.

There will be seasons where the baby will be the centre of everyone's attention and when our wives will be consumed with the process of nurturing a young dependant life. Then there will be seasons where we can have more time together.

The wisdom comes in knowing what season we are in. If we try to fight against a season we will be like a farmer trying to reap a harvest in winter. Ecclesiastes promises us there is a season for everything"

> *"For everything there is a season, a time for every activity under heaven."*
>
> Ecclesiastes 3:1

Justin—this is the season

"I did my best to understand the physical, emotional and mental changes that went on with my wife (nesting instincts, baby shows and baby shopping) so I could know how to support her the best I could. Complimenting her became more and more difficult as she swelled up. Obviously, intimate times were also more difficult.

"I realised that I was not in control of the process. The birth plans we made were good (birthing centre, 100% natural, water birth), but I also had to be prepared for the eventuality that things may not go according to our plans. In our case, one week before the birth, we were told we could not have a water birth or go to the birthing centre because of pre-eclampsia.

"This confused us, as we had prayed and asked God for everything to be as my wife wanted, but it never happened that way. That last week was pretty stressful at times and we had lots of talks and prayer, trusting God was in control, especially when we knew what was possible with pre-eclampsia.

"I also had the responsibility of caring for my wife and son once he was born. At one point my wife was surrounded by fifteen friends and family who had come to visit us soon after the birth. In hindsight, this was too much for her and I should have stepped in.

"Being a husband and father is a huge responsibility. But don't feel weighed down by this, trust that God will help you to be the best that you can for your family."

> *"Trust in the Lord with all your heart; do not depend on your own understanding. Seek His will in all you do, and He will show you which path to take."*
>
> Proverbs 3:5–6

The journey of pregnancy for a man, although different to a woman, is just as important. Enjoy the experience and work together with your wife to make the pregnancy as enjoyable as possible. Through this you will build a strong family. Above all things, keep God at the centre of your family.

For Personal Reflection

For the mother:

Have you expressed to your husband what kind of support you would like during pregnancy and labour?

Think of three things that will make your husband a great dad and tell him

For the father:

What are your concerns as you approach parenthood?

What are you looking forward to?

What will need to change in your life when your baby comes?

How are you fulfilling your role as the spiritual head of your home and the prayer covering for your family?

13

Preparing Siblings For The New Baby

"I will teach all your children, and they will enjoy great peace."

Isaiah 54:13

Get ready

Well done! You survived baby number one. You've probably learnt to do three things at once. You've may have discovered new definitions of exhausted. You may long for the day when you can go to the toilet without being interrupted!

I remember lying cuddling my firstborn whilst heavily pregnant with Simeon, my second child, thinking, *how could I possibly love another child as much as I've loved Josh my first?* It's amazing how love does take over when you first set eyes on your newborn child.

The next concern I had was how we could avoid sibling jealousy for the new arrival. This chapter is all about reassuring older siblings, so that they know they are still loved, and to help them find their new place in the new, expanded family.

A new arrival in the house can be a stressful event for an older sibling. If they are the firstborn, they will have had our undivided attention since birth. Now someone else is coming along who wants to share that attention. As a result, we won't be able to pick them up whenever they want. We may not be able to answer their questions immediately. Sometimes games will have to be put on hold while we see to the new arrival. All this can be quite frustrating for the older sibling. The new baby can be viewed as a threat instead of a joy.

To begin with, the baby doesn't want to play football (indeed "Mummy tells me off whenever I throw the football in their direction"). To a toddler, it can seem like all a baby does is cry, have dirty nappies and take up Mummy's time.

We need God's creative heart to give us inspiration as we raise our children, each with their own unique personalities. Here are a few ideas we've picked up along the way through having our five children.

Pre-birth

Let them enjoy the experience of how amazing God is in the creation of their new brother or sister. Websites like www.babycentre.co.uk can give you a weekly update on what is happening in the womb. We have used such sites to share pictures with our children each week, so that they know how big their brother or sister is. We have printed the pictures off the Internet and put them up on their wall and they have proudly shown these pictures to their friends, pointing out how big the new baby is in Mummy's tummy.

Tell them, "It's your baby too..." so that they can begin thinking about the adjustments they will make as this new person arrives in the world, who they have a role in looking after. It will give them a real sense of ownership and responsibility.

Let them come along to baby scans so that they can also see their new baby growing and moving and maybe 'waving' at them. Grab a picture at the end of the scan and involve them in working out which bit of the picture is their new sibling's head, hands and feet. Remind them that God is creating their sibling just as He made them.

Include them in everything... from buying clothes, to choosing a name. Pray together as a family for which name God wants for the new baby. Include all members of the family in this process. Of course, make it clear that Mummy and Daddy have the last say, but make it fun and allow them to be a part of it.

We have had some strange and funny suggestions so far. Let's just say that 'Pom-Pom' never made it onto our top ten possible names for the new baby. But our children felt involved in the process and now that they are older we are able to laugh together about some of the suggestions they made.

Pray together for your unborn child. Encourage your child to lay hands on your tummy and pray for your unborn child. Listen carefully to what they say. It's amazing how God can use a child to speak powerful words of prophecy over your unborn child.

A two-year-old girl went up to a lady in church and said, "You have two babies in your tummy." She then skipped off to do something else. The next week the lady discovered she was pregnant and nine months later she gave birth... to twins!

Choose a special Bible verse together for them to use with their unborn baby. They can say it or pray it over the baby when they have been born. They could even use it to make a decoration to put over the baby's cot or in the baby's room.

Let them help make the baby's cot ready for baby's arrival and help choose which toys to put in it. If the baby has a room to themselves ask your toddler what special things to put in the room for their newborn sibling.

If they have been sleeping in the cot until now, make the transition to big boy or girl bed a few months before the new baby arrives, so they can get used to being in their new bed and won't feel like they are being pushed out of their cot by the newborn baby.

Get the photo album out. Look at photos of your first born from when they were a baby. Show them how small they were and how Mummy and Daddy or someone was always holding them. Talk about how they were not able to do much on their own to begin with, but now that they have grown they can do more. This will help them to know what to expect. It will also mean that if they are disappointed because their baby cannot yet hold a car or a doll, they will know that this is something they'll be able to do when they are older.

Give them crayons and paper so that they can think about what their baby will look like. Talk about what things they will be able to do with their baby straight away. For example, they may be able to cuddle them with Mummy and Daddy, or help bathe the baby.

Go out to the shops with your child for them to go and buy a present for their newborn sibling. This could be something practical or maybe they can be the one to buy them their first Bible.

Post birth

When you first see your other children after the new baby is born, make sure you give them lots of attention even if you don't feel 100% yourself. They have probably missed you and their routine may have been disrupted with no Mummy or Daddy around for a time. Introduce them to their new baby brother or sister.

Arrange a special card and present for the older sibling from your new baby.

Get your friends on board to help you. When our second son arrived, our eldest son, Joshua, was 18 months old. Lots of visitors came to see the new baby. When they arrived I asked them to spend time with Joshua first, before they had cuddles with the newborn, so that Joshua would not feel left out. It made a world of difference in the bonding process between new baby and sibling.

Make sure you have quality one-on-one time with your toddler when your newborn is asleep. Read stories, play games, dance to songs, do art and craft, and have some special activities put aside for those precious moments. Get a Spy Kit from Children Can and play it as you pray together and do the puzzles together. Be creative in your tiredness. Snuggle up and watch a DVD together. They will appreciate that one-on-one time together.

Get them involved in everything you do with the baby. They can help bathe and dry the baby, hold wipes during nappy changes and even choose which clothes their brother/sister is going to wear that day. This last idea has been a firm favourite with my children, as they present their baby sibling to the rest of the family each day in the clothes they have chosen. The baby doesn't mind if they are not looking the height of fashion, even if you might!

Encourage them to pray for "their baby"… maybe in your family prayer times. You can even get the baby to lay hands on their big sibling and 'pray' for them. Obviously, you will have to put on a special voice for the baby but the older sibling will love it!

Make sure your baby also kisses and cuddles them goodnight. Why not lie them next to your child and allow them to gently hug and kiss them too. This ends the day on a positive note for both your children.

With each child you will see differences in their character and temperament, but know that God is in it. Look for ways you can enhance the positives and turn around the negatives for God's glory. In the long run siblings should end up the best of friends. Even when their friends have left them or they have lost contact with them, they will always have their brothers and sisters with shared childhood history. That is worth nurturing to see how their destinies will work together for God's glory.

All of this is about valuing and showing value to every member of the family. God values the weakest and most vulnerable members of society and this is something we can teach older siblings as they learn to gently love.

If there is any sibling rivalry, don't panic. This does not spell disaster for your family. Instead, be clear about your expectations for their behaviour and talk it through with God.

For Personal Reflection

Have you discussed the baby's arrival
with your other children,
including what the baby will be able to do
when they are first born?

Have you encouraged your other children
to pray for the baby?

Encourage your children to choose a Bible verse
or a Bible story that they would like
to share with their new baby.

Part 3
Preparing for Baby's Birth

14

Three in the Birthing Room

"A person standing alone can be attacked and defeated, but two can stand back-to-back and conquer. Three are even better, for a triple-braided cord is not easily broken."

Ecclesiastes 4:12

God, the senior partner

Your first time in labour will be full of unknowns. No matter how much you have read about it or how many classes you've attended, it will only be when you have experienced labour that you will know what to expect. Even then, each subsequent labour can be very different.

Amidst the excitement of giving birth there can be an underlying anxiety—the not knowing exactly what will happen (or sheer panic at the thought of what is to come). Will I recognise when I've gone into labour? When should I get to the hospital? Will I get there in time?

The solution to anxiety and fear is to trust God. Only God knows the exact time when He is ready for your child to make their entrance into the world. This is when the partnership with you, God and your partner needs to be strong. Don't leave God outside in the waiting room. He most definitely wants to be present with His presence in the birthing room, whether that is at home, in hospital, or elsewhere.

So how can you bring God into the delivery room?

Trust that God has heard, and will put into action, everything you have prayed for during the pregnancy.

All you have read so far will hopefully have started to help you prepare, mentally and spiritually, for your new addition. Soak yourself in God's Word. If those moments of anxiety or concern come, go straight to God's Word for reassurance. This helped me to get my mind straight. It is also what allowed God to be in partnership with myself and my husband through all our pregnancies.

God was there even before your baby was a twinkle in your eye, ordering their steps, planning their life, creating and knitting them together powerfully and intricately, positioning them in the right family—your family. God knew the plans He had in store for your child even before they were conceived. He knows how your child will be used by Him to see His kingdom come and His will be done. He knows the way they will look, what giftings they will have. He knows their character, their personality and how He will nurture that through you as parents to see them glorify His name. Your child is in His hands.

God worked in the creation of your child in the womb, as one cell separated into many cells, as each DNA strand was knit together, as the fingers and toes budded and the facial features were created. The eyes, ears and the digestive system, the heart and all the internal organs came together under His watchful eye. God has joyously seen all His creativity unleashed upon your child. So God wants to continue being at the centre when you are in labour.

My second pregnancy

My second pregnancy started with a bump, as I doubled up in the toilets at work unable to move. I was taken to the hospital where I was found to have low blood pressure. They also did a test to check for pregnancy. To my surprise and delight I was pregnant. 'Grace and Favour' was on the way.

The rest of the pregnancy was relatively uneventful, except for a little bit of bleeding around the 6 month mark, but God was in control of this baby coming.

I considered having a water birth, but decided not to on this occasion. As my first contractions started I felt we had plenty of time to get to the hospital and I noticed that we were a little short of food in the house, so suggested we go shopping. Perhaps a walk around the supermarket would help speed up the labour.

As we walked around I could feel the contractions growing in intensity, so we quickly paid and left. I felt God saying we had time to drop the groceries at home, which we did before arriving in the hospital.

At the hospital we had a lovely midwife who looked after us, but I felt that Simeon would not be born till after 8pm that evening. Just before Simeon was born the midwives changed shifts and in came this wonderful midwife who loved Jesus.

Simeon had been waiting for a Christian to deliver him. She suggested I try the stool (a seat with hole in the middle). As I sat on it my waters broke like a flood and two pushes later Simeon came out, full of black hair and looking gorgeous! God arranged the midwife care wonderfully and His timing was perfect.

I have often said (to people's raised eyebrows) that the labour has been the highlight and the best part of pregnancy for me. Going into each one I had with the reassurance that God was with me and that He would be holding my hand, just like my husband, throughout the labour.

I've found labour to be as much a spiritual experience as it is a physical one. With each labour I had to get into *the zone*, focusing on the job at hand of delivering another beautiful child, but also ensuring that God was with me. It's easy to lose that focus in the intensity of labour.

With all of my labours, even though my husband has been physically there as an amazing support, rubbing my back and holding my hand tight when needed, the partnership between myself and God has been the most important thing. The simple revelation that God was with me helped me.

Karen's testimony—God's appointed time

"I was pregnant with twins. The doctors were worried about the way the twins were positioned so they booked me to have a caesarean section before my due date. As I prayed, my desire for a normal delivery grew. My one prayer to God was, 'Let these babies be born at the appointed time.'

"Two days before the caesarean had been booked, I went into spontaneous labour. I delivered both babies naturally and everything went smoothly. Praise God!"

The pain of childbirth

Let's be clear that the pain in childbirth is a curse. When Adam and Even sinned in the garden of Eden, God spoke this curse over Eve in Genesis 3:16:

> *"Then He said to the woman, 'I will sharpen the pain of your pregnancy, and in pain you will give birth. And you will desire to control your husband, but he will rule over you.'"*

When Jesus died on the cross He became a curse for us. Since the time of Adam until the time of Christ, intimacy with God had been at arm's length. In the temple, a curtain separated the most holy place from the rest of the temple. It was in this place where God symbolically dwelt. Only one person, the high priest, was allowed behind the curtain. He was only allowed there once a year and on condition that he brought a sacrifice for his own sins and the sin of the people.

When Jesus died on the cross the battle that began in Eden was declared finished (John 19:30). At that moment Jesus became a sacrifice once for all time. Annual sacrifices were no longer needed (Hebrews 7:27).

When God spoke the curse over the serpent in Genesis 3:15 He said,

> *"And I will cause hostility between you and the woman, and between your offspring and her offspring. He will strike your head, and you will strike his heel."*

Jesus trampled on the serpent's head at this moment.

> *"But Christ has rescued us from the curse pronounced by the law. When He was hung on the cross, He took upon Himself the curse for our wrongdoing. For it is written in the Scriptures, 'Cursed is everyone who is hung on a tree.' Through Christ Jesus, God has blessed the Gentiles with the same blessing He promised to Abraham, so that we who are believers might receive the promised Holy Spirit through faith".*
>
> Galatians 3:13–14

So Jesus swapped our curse for His blessing. This opens the potential for a completely pain free labour. In the same way as healing is available through Jesus' death and resurrection, so too is a pain free labour. Some women have experienced this as they have believed God by faith.

Others have believed it and found labour to be bearable, though with a degree of discomfort. Either way, this is not a failure. Just as God heals some sick people but not all, we live with the same tension here. This tension will only be fully resolved when Christ returns. At that time Revelation 22:3 tells us, *"no longer will there be a curse upon anything."*

I encourage you to believe God for a pain free birth. Study the Scriptures and pray. At the same time, be reassured that for centuries people have delivered babies and coped with the pain and today, with modern analgesics, things are better than they once were. If you experience pain in labour this is not a failure, take pain killers and know that the labour will be short-lived. God leads each of us in different ways. Trust God and believe Him for His best. Either way childbirth is a divine miracle.

So, giving birth, what should you expect?

Your body is going through things that it may not have gone through before, so initially each contraction can be a bit of a shock. Contractions tend to start gently and build in intensity, before settling into a rhythm or pattern that you can work with. It's a feeling you've never experienced until now, but God has made you an amazing woman and He has everything under control in the labour room, even down to the people who will be at hand to help deliver your child. Trust God, trust the people who God has placed around you to facilitate the birth, and make it your aim to try and enjoy that miraculous experience of child birth.

Remember, you are blessed beyond the curse. You can have a labour like the Hebrew woman: quick and easy. But as with all things, don't let presumption take over faith in this. God is exceedingly, abundantly able to do all things and you may be surprised at how easy labour can be. But He also asks us to use wisdom. In other words, look for God's best and trust God with the rest! He will guide you through.

The best partnership that you could have in the labour room is the three-cord strand that is not easily broken. That's you, your partner and God. The joy of child birth is an amazing miracle, something to be totally wondered at. It brings many emotions to a woman (and a man) that they have never experienced before—especially the totally overwhelming feeling that they have played a part in the creation of a new human being.

Many midwives who have delivered hundreds of babies still experience the awe of the child birth experience. It is one of God's miracles and shows what an awesome God we serve. No one could have created our bodies with such intricacies by accident. Too much thought has been put into everything. God has brought your child to you. Now it is time to enjoy a lifetime together.

Your spiritual birth plan

There are many things you can do to put God at the centre whilst you are in labour. Not every idea will be right for every person. If I had given birth with my husband reading Scriptures out loud next to me, I would have been more likely to throw something at him, rather than thank him for his great words of edification at my time of need. That would have built my frustration, not my faith and trust in God. I was focusing completely on seeing my child come into the world swiftly and safely.

As you prepare for your labour you will probably write a birth plan, detailing the things you would like to see happen. All of this helps you to prepare, even if the plans change later on. In the same way, why not write a spiritual birth plan? Here are some ideas for things you may want to include in your spiritual birth plan as you write your thoughts on paper.

Prayer chains. Prepare a prayer chain for when you go into labour. Ask people in advance if they would be prepared to pray for you at that time. I set up group contacts on my phone for all who had agreed to be pray for me so that I could send out one text when I went into labour. These prayers bring God's peace into the labour room.

> *"Don't worry about anything; instead, pray about everything. Tell God what you need, and thank Him for all He has done. Then you will experience God's*

*peace, which exceeds anything we can understand.
His peace will guard your hearts and minds as you
live in Christ Jesus."*

Philippians 4:6–7

Because of the sense of God's peace in the labour room, I have had midwives comment on how easy it has been to deliver some of my children. Of course, there is always time for your partner to pray for you and the baby during labour.

Words of faith. Whilst you are in labour, speak words of faith to yourself. Find verses that are easy to remember like Philippians 4:13—*"For I can do everything through Christ, who gives me strength."* Or remind yourself that, "God is good, all the time." For some labour will be easy. For others it will be more intense. Either way, having some words of faith to hand will help you to keep your focus on God as you go through labour.

Your environment. Create an environment that will help you to connect with God. If you enjoy worship music, put some worship tracks into your birthing bag or create a playlist for labour on your iPod.

If you have a picture that has inspired you in your walk with God, take a copy with you in your hospital bag.

During birth, don't be afraid to ask for lighting to be changed, or even people to be moved until you are comfortable with the environment. Make that room your own personal sanctuary for as long as you are there, dedicating the space to God.

The first act after birth. Consider and discuss with your partner what you would like to do together as soon as your baby is born. Many parents plan to pray for their baby as soon as is practical. Some parents desire to anoint their baby with oil or read a specific scripture over their life as they welcome into the world. Planning in advance can help you to be prepared with anything you may need and adds to the significance of the occasion.

Let God be God. The range of emotions you will go through during labour will be immense and sometimes the pressure we put on ourselves as women to have the perfect birth experience, especially as a Christian, can be huge. But if we can let go and let God be God, even when things don't go according to our plans, we will find His peace.

> *"We can make our plans, but the Lord determines our steps."*
>
> Proverbs 16:9

When we have this mind set it is easier to know that God has everything under control, even if it doesn't fit with what we originally planned.

Pregnancy number five

My previous pregnancy had ended with a miscarriage, so I was a little apprehensive at the start of this pregnancy. I gave my little one to God straight away, knowing that He knew what was best for me as a mother and for us as a family. 'Faithful Jewel' was a wriggler and had a very uneventful time in the womb, growing and getting ready for the real world. My children (three boys at this stage) were all excited as they waited for the new baby.

Faithful Jewel was a healthy, happy baby in utero. It came to 41 weeks and they seemed happy to stay put. I got bigger and bigger—bigger than I had ever been—then eventually the day came for him to arrive. We went into hospital and two and a half hours later Benjamin was born via water birth. God blessed me with this pregnancy and labour. I was continually aware that He was in control.

For Personal Reflection

Write a spiritual birth plan

Make a list of people who would be willing to pray for you when labour begins

Use the declarations in part 4 as you prepare yourself to go into the labour room with God

15

The Perfect Labour?

It's your story

My counsel to all ladies who are pregnant or hoping to conceive is this: do not listen to other people's stories unless it is one that will build your faith during pregnancy. It is natural that people will want to share their experiences with you, since they've already been through it, but that does not mean it will be helpful to you.

I have met and counselled women who, after listening to people's horror stories about pregnancy and labour, have developed such a strong fear of pregnancy that they have determined to never get pregnant. What we feed our minds prior to pregnancy and leading up to labour is very important.

The reality of childbirth is that it is something which God has given and that God is in charge of. The world has conditioned us regarding what we should expect during labour and pregnancy. By watching the documentaries and dramas shown on TV that depict the childbirth experience (where, for dramatic effect, they often show the worst case scenarios of childbirth) we can become completely overawed. This can so easily get in the way of us keeping our eyes focused on our God, who has blessed us from the curse.

Each person's story is different and you will have yours, but whatever happens, know that every child is infinitely special to God. As we lean on God during our time of pregnancy our relationship with Him can only get stronger. We can see Him watching over us, intervening where necessary and turning things around. We can see His hand on ours and our baby's life.

God wants to be involved in your story. Turn to Him and hear His heart for your unborn child. The story of your birth and labour is ordered by Him and, as most of us know, sometimes our ways are not God's ways. His plan and story always turns out the best.

Our third child

During my third pregnancy everything seemed to be going well without complications. But for some reason I was filled with fears which I had not experienced in my other pregnancies. The focus of my fear was death: either mine or my unborn baby's. I shared these fears with my husband and we focused in prayer, laying hands on 'Jubilee Destiny' and speaking life and health into them.

Every check was coming up clear, but there was still the niggling feeling that I really had to baton down the hatches and pray for this one. My husband was also praying against death independently from me, not wanting to feed my fears.

Another family in our church had felt the same urge to pray regularly and urgently for our pregnancy. They kept their prayers to themselves until Jubilee Destiny had been born.

Jubilee Destiny was very happy inside the womb, seemed very peaceful, but was moving enough to keep me happy. The night before my 40-week appointment I started to feel contractions. We called the grandparents to come and watch the children as we prepared to go to the hospital. We asked our intercessors to pray and sat down to eat. It felt like we had time.

Then everything stopped.

An hour and a half later, Granny walked in surprised that we were just sat quite peacefully, chatting. She had expected us to rush out the door to the hospital, but it turned out to be a false labour.

Granny decided to stay the night, just in case. The next day I went to my 40-week appointment and explained what had happened. A lovely Irish midwife was on duty and checked that everything was how it should be. She offered to get me started with a sweep, but I had always wanted to start naturally, so declined.

By the time we had arrived home I was in full blown labour. We turned around and went straight back to the hospital. The same midwife was on duty. I requested a water birth (highly recommended!) and she managed to get me in just as my waters broke. The midwife was wonderful and supportive, rubbing my back and encouraging me, telling me how amazing I was being. Ninety minutes later, with four strong pushes, Matthew came out.

The cord was wrapped around his neck three times and there was a true knot in the chord (a potentially fatal complication). He looked blue and limp. The midwife cut the cord quickly and rushed him to resuscitation. Olly asked if he should go with our baby and I was left alone in the labour room by myself.

A tremendous peace came over me as I said out loud to God, "He's in your hands." I knew he was alright. God was in this. I knew He was looking after my baby. Before they could get Matthew to the oxygen, he had already pinked up and had a good cry. God was in charge!

My miracle boy was alive. God had prompted us to pray and he had survived against the odds. The fact that I had gone into false labour meant that my body was limbered up for a very quick delivery the next day. God had ordained everything so that Matthew could be delivered alive and well.

Because of the speed of the delivery I haemorrhaged heavily. The midwife and doctor were quick to spot it and intervened.

God had positioned the right people, with the right experience and gifting to ensure that Matthew would live out the destiny God had ordained for him. He was called Jubilee Destiny in the womb because we believe that God will use him to bring many people to salvation, finding freedom and their destiny in God. No wonder the enemy was not keen on his survival. But God overruled Satan's plans.

When you trust that God is in charge, His peace will reside with you during the birth—no matter what!

What? A caesarean!

This book is not written to make you feel guilty if things don't go how you expect. In some circles caesarean births have bad connotations attached to them. But God is in charge of the details of your pregnancy, labour and ultimately of your child. He knows the call and destiny on your children's lives. If your birth is not a 'normal' birth, continue holding onto God.

I have spoken to many ladies who feel they failed as a woman in labour because they didn't have a vaginal birth. The most important thing is that your child has been brought safely into this world. God has given medical professionals knowledge and they often know when they need to intervene quickly during the labour process. Trust and allow God to use these people for the safe delivery of our children.

My sister felt like she had failed in her role of giving birth as she was under anaesthetic when they delivered my niece by forceps delivery. She was not awake during the delivery and she felt she had missed out on seeing her little girl being born. But baby Hannah was born safely to a mum who is a fabulous mother.

Hannah now loves praying with her mummy and loves Jesus. She is a little girl whose life was saved to fulfil her destiny in God. The same goes for caesarean sections. As a parent, know that your unborn child has an amazing destiny planned by God, just like Josiah in the Bible who from the age of just 8 was ruling a nation. So in the delivery room set your thoughts on the things of God and get ready to see your child come safely into the world.

You can have a great story of a child delivered safely, a God who placed the right medical professionals around you, and a child's destiny and call in progress!

Sonya—4 children, 4 caesareans

"I have finally (one week before my fourth caesarean section) come to some conclusions that gave me peace. For at least three different reasons I am unable to vaginally deliver my children. Thank God that He has made another way for me to still experience the joy of having these children. Thank the Lord that with each birth He has brought me closer to Him and given me a greater awareness of myself. Thank the Lord that I have had such wide and varied birth experiences and the gift of a wonderful day in peaceful, enjoyable labour—something not usual for ladies who have caesarean births. Thank the Lord for the gifts, skills and talents of my surgeons, without whom I wouldn't have any children or may not even be here myself.

"I will never know why my births have happened this way, but I know that I can trust God that He is showing me a way through in victory."

Naima's testimony—disaster, disappointment and God

"At the end of my first pregnancy I needed an emergency caesarean section under general anaesthetic and also required a blood transfusion. Having been through this, my one prayer for my next pregnancy was to have a natural delivery and for things to be normal, but the concerns and anxiety still lingered.

"I joined a womb ministry and each month I was completely elevated as prayers were answered and I just knew that God was in control. It was a forum in which anything could be talked about; money, pains, emotions and relationships were all discussed. The team never judged but steered us towards the promises of God and any negative fears started to drift away.

"In the end I had Gordon by elective caesarean section. When this decision was made I was very tearful. I felt that yet again the true magnificence of labour would be stolen from me. As I spoke with others I was reassured that this was perhaps God's plan for me and I just didn't know why yet. How true this proved to be.

"When the surgeons opened me up they discovered a lot of scar tissue, which they believe came from an infection following the first C-section. My uterus had thinned. Had I not had an elective caesarean it would probably have ended up as another emergency caesarean section. Straight away I knew that God had intervened, not only to clean up previous errors, but also to save me from what would have been traumatic for me."

Wherever you look, if you have kept God the focus of your pregnancy and labour you will see God's hand in it. Trust Him with the details.

For Personal Reflection

Take time to soak in God's presence
and trust Him with the details

16

When Baby Arrives

Taking charge of your spiritual walk

When your baby is first born, life will be busy. There will be a whole new way of life to get used to as you start your twenty-four hour a day labour of love. For the first week or so you will probably be occupied with recovering from pregnancy, labour and birth, learning to feed and bonding with your newborn—not to mention welcoming guests, answering phone calls to long distant relatives and snatching sleep where you can.

As a routine begins to settle in, start to think about how you can fit time with God into it all. For some people this will be a natural thing to do. For others, it will be something that you have to fight for.

Some simple ideas can go a long way to helping you get back on track and, for some, it will mean a change in the way you spend time with God. Before you may have been able to sit for an hour and listen to a sermon online. Now you will probably find that you rarely have an uninterrupted hour and, when you do, your body needs it to rest.

Build in set times to pause and pray throughout the week. This could be during feeding time or in the car on the way home from dropping older siblings at nursery or school.

Choose a Bible passage to meditate on each week. Make that passage the first thing you read each morning. Keep a Bible open at those verses somewhere in your kitchen, so you can be prompted to read them during a spare few minutes. Write the passage on a piece of paper and put in in your baby bag, so it's at hand wherever you go. Share the passage with your partner and make it the last thing you read at night time. In this way you will be able to think about this passage all week, even when you are not reading it.

If your latest addition has decided that 2.00am is the perfect time to play one night, you could use that time while you are up. Most of us are not at our best in the middle of the night, but if your sleep is going to be disturbed anyway, why not use the time to pray?

Taking charge of your baby's spiritual walk

God has His hands on our babies from the womb. When they are born He still wants to be involved in their lives! Imagine a baby so filled with the Holy Spirit being taken shopping with their mother. Whilst in the shop, a stranger comes and starts cooing over the baby. The stranger asks mum's permission and picks up the baby. As they do so, the Spirit of God in the baby works to convict the person of sin, righteousness and the coming judgment (John 16:8).

"I don't know what it is about your baby, but I feel so bad. I know I've done things wrong. I didn't think I was a bad person, but now I need to put things right with God."

The mum then leads the stranger to Jesus.

If this sounds far-fetched to you, look at the following scriptures to see how the Holy Spirit has worked in the past.

> *"As a result of the apostles' work, sick people were brought out into the streets on beds and mats so that Peter's shadow might fall across some of them as he went by."*
>
> Acts 5:15

> *"God gave Paul the power to perform unusual miracles. When handkerchiefs or aprons that had merely touched his skin were placed on sick people, they were healed of their diseases, and evil spirits were expelled."*
>
> Acts 19:11–12

Here we see an inanimate objects (a handkerchief) and a shadow (which is an absence of light) being linked to an anointed man of God performing miraculous signs. Yet the children and babies under our care are not inanimate objects or shadows. They are fully human and responsive to the Spirit of God.

In a newborn baby's brain there are around 100 billion neurons (brain cells). Links between these brain cells, called synapses, form at the rate of 3 billion per second in the early days, with an 8-month old having around 1000 trillion synaptic connections. These links are reinforced by the input we give to our children. But this rate of growth does not last. At the age of two, no more synapses are made. At age 10 the brain removes the weakest links where there has been no information. Around half of the synapses are removed at this time. These then stay the same until the age of 70, when in some cases they are gradually removed.[5]

The right time to introduce children to God, so that their knowledge of Him can grow, is when they are young, encouraging the God-synapses to grow. This will set them up for the future. Many adults testify of how early childhood experiences have affected the rest of their lives. Perhaps they did well and were praised for their efforts? Perhaps they saw God do a miracle? Perhaps they were laughed at in front of the rest of the family? Perhaps other siblings, for valid reasons, were given more attention than them? Perhaps they experienced bereavement in the family? We are shaping the adults of the future as we introduce our children to God and expose them to a life with Him.

Moses (Exodus 2:1–10)

When Moses is born in Egypt, Pharaoh puts out an order that all male baby Israelites should be killed. Moses' mother refuses to let this be her son's fate, so she places him in the river leaving his fate to God. Imagine her walking home slowly, praying for God to be merciful.

When she got home she may have wept or busied herself cleaning. In her heart she would have known that she would never see her son again (and if she did see him, she probably would not even recognise him).

Meanwhile, Pharaoh's daughter finds the child in the river and has compassion on him. Moses' sister, Miriam, suggests that she goes to find a lady who can nurse the child at the breast (formula milk had not yet been invented) and so Moses is reunited with his mother.

---

[5] Data taken from pp. 26–28 of *How to Raise a Brighter Child* by Joan Beck.

She breast feeds him until he is weaned (in Bible times this was around the age of three or four) and then he grows up in Pharaoh's palace. We know that Moses' mother was a godly woman. Hebrews 11:23 tells us that she hid him from Pharaoh for three months by faith.

As a godly woman, she would not simply have been sitting their breast feeding. She had received her child back from the dead! God had redeemed him. Not only that, but God was providing for her family through the payments Pharaoh's daughter would have made for her feeding services, and her son was guaranteed a privileged upbringing in the palace. She would not have been sitting there surfing TV channels looking for something decent to watch! Surely she would have been praying for Moses and prophesying over his life:

"Moses, God has rescued you for a purpose. God has a destiny for your life. Pharaoh's daughter called you 'Moses'—the drawn out one. May God use you to draw us out from this slavery that demands the sweat of our adults and the blood of our children."

When Moses was weaned from the breast his mother would have kissed him goodbye and given him over to Pharaoh's daughter. Yet the seed that she sowed and her continued prayers for him took root:

> *"It was by faith that Moses, when he grew up, refused to be called the son of Pharaoh's daughter. He chose to share the oppression of God's people instead of enjoying the fleeting pleasures of sin."*
>
> Hebrews 11:24–25

Moses chose to reject his upbringing, the way of the Egyptians, a life of privilege. Instead he chose to follow the way of his forefathers, associating with a nation of slaves. This is clearly linked with the call of God on his life. But how did God activate that call on his life? Surely his mother had something to do with it. A seed was deposited so securely in his life that it affected his life decisions. This is the glorious responsibility we have as we minister to our babies.

From those early years, our children will learn from our words and our example to walk in the ways of the Lord. Our prayer for them can be, like the prophet Samuel whose mother nurtured his faith when he was young and prayed for him, that having started in God's way, our children never depart from Him.

God can place an anointing on your child's life in the womb and you will see it played out when they are born.

The interceding baby

When our firstborn child, Joshua, was a baby we were part of a service where the Holy Spirit was moving. We prayed for him to be filled with the Holy Spirit and he started to laugh. As he laughed he reached out and touched a lady who was sitting near to us. She fell to the floor under the power of God. People looked on amazed: "Did you see that baby pray for that lady?"

Simeon, our second born son, was with us as we led an away day for primary school children to encounter God. We had taught about the Holy Spirit and were about to start praying for children who wanted more of God. Simeon was twelve months old and could only speak a few words, but at this point in the session he said very clearly: "The Holy Spirit is here." God came and met with the children who were there, as the adults stood open mouthed contemplating the majesty of God who spoke through a child who was only just finding his first words.

When our babies encounter God it is not cute, it is powerful. God says in Psalm 8:2:

> *"You have taught children and infants to tell of Your strength (to give You praise), silencing Your enemies and all who oppose You."*

What a privilege it is to minister to our little ones and see a strong foundation in their walk with God, even from before they are born.

> *"God chose things the world considers foolish in order to shame those who think they are wise. And He chose things that are powerless to shame those who are powerful."*
>
> 1 Corinthians 1:27

God's greatness is shown in His ability to use one so small and weak.

Included in the gathering of God's people

When God's people gather, the babies are included.

> *"Then Moses gave them this command: 'At the end of every seventh year, the Year of Release, during the Festival of Shelters, you must read this Book of Instruction to* **all** *the people of Israel when they assemble before the Lord your God at the place He chooses. Call them all together—men, women,* **children***, and the foreigners living in your towns—so they may hear this Book of Instruction and learn to fear the Lord your God and carefully obey all the terms of these instructions.'"*
>
> Deuteronomy 31:10–12

> *"Gather all the people—the elders, the children,* **and even the babies***. Call the bridegroom from his quarters and the bride from her private room."*
>
> Joel 2:16

> *"About 5,000 men were fed that day, in addition to all the women and* **children***!"*
>
> Matthew 14:21

> *"All the people assembled with a unified purpose at the square just inside the Water Gate. They asked Ezra the scribe to bring out the Book of the Law of Moses, which the Lord had given for Israel to obey. So on October 8 Ezra the priest brought the Book of the Law before the assembly, which included the men and women and* **all the children old enough to understand***. He faced the square just inside the Water Gate from early morning until noon and read aloud to everyone who could understand. All the people listened closely to the Book of the Law."*
>
> Nehemiah 8:1–3

At first glance this last passage looks like the youngest children have been excluded from the gathering, but there is more to this story than first meets the eye. Ezra and Nehemiah have been rebuilding the walls and the temple following the exile of the Israelites.

In the process of the buildings works they have found the book of the Law. As they read it, they realise that God promised they would be sent into exile if they did not obey His commandments and that God had kept His promise. They also saw that they were still living in sin. So Ezra called all the people of Jerusalem to hear the book of the Law read aloud. This was the first five books of our Old Testament.

All the men came. All the women came. All the children who were old enough to understand also came. This only left the babies and toddlers. No one was left to look after them, since the whole city was going to the gathering, so were the babies left home alone? No! Of course not, they would have been taken along too.

Not only that, but we have seen how a baby in the womb can respond to the Spirit of God. The babies in Nehemiah's time may not have understood every word of Leviticus as it was read, but they would have understood the spirit of unity that was in that place.

The point of this scripture is not to say that the babies were excluded from the gathering. Rather, it is to spell out that all people were expected to be there, listening at whatever level of understanding they were able, even down to the youngest child.

So expose your children to the presence of God. Take them to church to be with the gathering of God's people. Let them sit in on your times with God. Let them, *"taste and see that the Lord is good!"* (Psalm 34:8).

Further comment on the passing on of our faith to our children is outside the remit of this book, but we encourage you to read our book *At Home with God*. This book contains simple biblical principles for passing on our faith to our children, using lessons learnt from the Jewish faith.

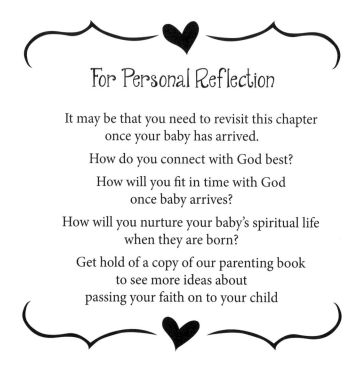

For Personal Reflection

It may be that you need to revisit this chapter
once your baby has arrived.

How do you connect with God best?

How will you fit in time with God
once baby arrives?

How will you nurture your baby's spiritual life
when they are born?

Get hold of a copy of our parenting book
to see more ideas about
passing your faith on to your child

17

Conclusion: Ministering to the Womb

God's plan for your baby

God has a purpose for our children, whilst they are still children. He wants to encounter them in the womb. God wants to pour His Spirit out onto them.

> *"Then, after doing all those things, I will pour out my Spirit upon all people."*
>
> Joel 2:28

> *"The earnest prayer of a righteous person has great power and produces wonderful results."*
>
> James 5:16

From those early years our children will learn from our words and our example to walk in the ways of the Lord. Our prayer for them can be that, like the prophet Samuel, having started in His way they will never depart from it.

> *"In the beginning the Word already existed."*
>
> John 1:1

Jesus is at the centre of every beginning, whether it is in the world or in your womb! He is the same yesterday, today and forever. God has ordained for your child, with their unique personality and calling, to be in your family at this time.

> *"…The Word was with God, and the Word was God. He existed in the beginning with God."*
>
> John 1:1–2

> *"God created everything through Him, and nothing was created except through Him."*
>
> John 1:3

Your child is a miracle of God's creation in action. Whatever the future has in store, know that God has good plans for you and your family.

A mother came to speak to me one day. "I gave my child a prophetic name and everything, and now they are causing me a complete nightmare—it didn't work!" In the same way, Mary must have wondered how things would work out with Jesus. She had received prophetic words, angelic visitations and divine introductions in those early days, but there were definitely times when she was ready to tear her hair out. Imagine finding your son, after he's been missing for several days, only for him to look at you and say, "Isn't it obvious where I was?" But whatever trials Mary faced (and which parent doesn't) she held onto all these things that had been spoken over her pregnancy and around the time of His birth.

> *"But Mary kept all these things in her heart and thought about them often."*
>
> Luke 2:19

It wasn't until much later in her life that she was able to fully understand how marvellously God had worked through her and her son Jesus.

As God is creating your child in your womb, He may reveal to you things about them that will take decades to be fulfilled. The principles in this book do not promise that you will have the perfect child—they will still have to walk their own journey through life. But whatever happens hang on in there! Hold on to the word God gives you concerning them and in due time you will see it come to pass. Remember the things God has spoken to you about your children, treasure them, pray them through and God will answer. Any season your children go through is not a life sentence. The only word that will last over your child is the one that God speaks.

God's plan for you

As you are pregnant and preparing to give birth, God does not want you to have any fear. He wants to walk this journey with you.

Prepare your mind and your spirit. Develop a spiritual birth plan and trust God. Let this whole season be one where you grow close to Him.

When labour begins, hold on to God and try to enjoy the experience.

As one lady said to me, "I was so glad you told me not to go into the labour experience with feelings of dread or fear, but with the aim of enjoying it. I had the most amazing birth experience. People who I tell don't believe me, but it is true: labour can be enjoyed and I am looking forward to my next pregnancy because of that."

As the season of pregnancy comes to an end, the season of parenting begins. May God's grace and wisdom be with you as you enjoy nurturing, learning about and spending time with your children.

> *"How joyful are those who fear the Lord—all who follow His ways!… Your children will be like vigorous young olive trees as they sit around your table."*
>
> Psalm 128:1 & 3

For Personal Reflection

What things has God spoken to you about your child?

How are you going to treasure these things in your heart?

Have you written these things down?

Part 4
Prayers and Declarations

Birth Declaration

Scriptural Confessions For Pregnancy and Delivery

Heavenly Father, I thank You for the fruit of the womb and the privilege of bringing Your baby, [baby's prophetic name], into the world (Psalm 127:3).

I thank You that You are the Lord, my shepherd. Therefore, my body will not be in want of all it needs to carry this pregnancy till the appointed time and baby [baby's prophetic name] will not be in want of all s/he needs for full and appropriate development (Psalm 23:1).

According to Your Word in Galatians 1:15, at the perfect time, when it pleases You, You will separate baby [baby's prophetic name] from my womb. Therefore, I line up with Your Word and declare that I shall not suffer miscarriage and the number of my days You will fulfil (Exodus 23:26). Baby [baby's prophetic name] will be born at the time You have ordained.

Father, I thank You that Your thoughts towards baby [baby's prophetic name] and me are of good and not evil, but to bring us to an expected end (Jeremiah 29:11). To this end we stand on Your Word and declare that the expected end of this pregnancy will be the safe delivery of a perfect and healthy child. On the day of their birth, Your joy will be our strength (Nehemiah 8:10) and I shall not labour in vain nor have trouble bringing forth, for baby [baby's prophetic name] and I are blessed of the Lord (Isaiah 65:23). Furthermore, I am assured that baby [baby's prophetic name] is good and perfect because You the Father of lights in whom there is no variation or shadow of turning, who gives good and perfect gifts (James 1:17).

As Your child, confident in Your Word and faithfulness, I allow the peace of God to rule in my heart and I refuse to worry about anything concerning this pregnancy and the safe delivery of baby [baby's prophetic name] (Colossians 3:15). I take authority over the spirit of fear and doubt and declare that I operate under the spirit of love, power and sound mind given to me by You (2 Timothy 1:7). I also bring into captivity every thought, imaginations and every high thing that wants to exalt itself against Your word (2 Corinthians 10:5).

My dear heavenly Father, I give You all the praise and glory for I know that just as You separated me from my mother's womb and have upheld me from birth (Psalm 71:6), You will do the same for baby [baby's prophetic name]. Thank You, Lord, for perfecting all that concerns me during this pregnancy through to baby [baby's prophetic name]'s delivery (Psalm 138:8).

Amen.

Baby Declaration

Prayer Scriptures For Your Baby

Dearest [baby's prophetic name],

You are God's gift. (Psalm 127:3)

You are a good and perfect gift. (James 1:17)

God knows everything about you now and everything about your future. (Psalm 139:1–5)

In fact, before you were conceived God knew you. (Jeremiah 1:4–5)

God formed your inward parts and covers you in the womb. (Psalm 139:13)

You have been fearfully and wonderfully made. (Psalm 139:14)

You are not a mistake, God knows all about you. (Psalm 139:15–16)

God knows even the number of hairs on your head. (Mathew 10:30)

He will bring you out of the womb at the time that pleases Him. (Galatians 1:15)

He has determined the exact time of your birth and where you will live. (Acts 17:26)

You will be upheld from birth by Him. (Psalm 71:6)

You are His offspring and it is in Him you live, move and have your being. (Acts 17:28)

The Lord is your shepherd, therefore you shall not want. (Psalm 23:1)

God's thoughts toward you is to give you a future and hope. (Jeremiah 29:11)

God loves you with an everlasting love. (Jeremiah 31:3)

The Lord will quiet you with His love and rejoice over you with singing. (Zephaniah 3:17)

No evil nor any plagues shall befall you, for His angels are watching over you. (Psalm 91:11)

Surely goodness and mercy will follow you all the days of your life and you will dwell in the house of the Lord forever. (Psalm 23:6)

You will seek God while you are young. (2 Chronicles 34:3)

You are amongst a generation that will never bow the knee to Baal. (1 Kings 19:18)

You are an arrow in the hands of the Lord. (Psalm 127:4)

You will do what is right in God's sight and walk in His ways all the days of your life. (2 Kings 22:2)

You will stand for the Lord and because of your witness you will see many people diligently serve God throughout your life. (2 Chronicles 34:33)

Prayers Against Fear

Here are a few fears that some women may come across. We have tried to give some practical and spiritual pointers. Please use the prayers below as a vehicle to get your mind straight before God. If you have chosen a name for your child whilst they are in the womb, use that name where indicated to make the prayer personal to you. Prayers are not like magic potions to get what you want, but are a conversation between you and the Living God—a God who loves you and also knows the best for you.

- You will find sections on the following fears:
- I'll have a miscarriage.
- I'll eat or drink the wrong thing and harm my baby
- I'm too stressed out. I'm worried, it's hurting the baby
- My baby will have a birth defect
- I'll go into labour too early and end up giving birth by myself
- I'll have complications like pre-eclampsia or gestational diabetes
- Labour will be too tough or painful. I'll never make it through
- I'm not going to be a good parent
- Other fears not covered above

The fear: I'll have a miscarriage

Most pregnancies result in healthy babies (less than 20 percent end in miscarriage). After your doctor can see a heartbeat (usually around 6–8 weeks) the risk of miscarriage drops to about 5 percent. And there's very reassuring news if you should have one. The odds of having a second miscarriage are very small, less than 3 percent. God has blessed me with 6 pregnancies and my heart goes out to anyone who has been through a miscarriage, as I know the emotional pain that goes along with that. But I also know God is a God of love and life and His blessings are bountiful. Trust Him.

> *"Dear Lord, You know me and know my unborn child. I love baby [baby's prophetic name] so much, but I am concerned for their life even in the womb. I worship you as my God and the Giver of life. You promise in your Word, in Exodus 23 verse 25–26, 'I will take away sickness from among you, and none will miscarry or be barren in your land. I will give you a full life span.' I claim that promise for my own life and my unborn baby's life now. I love You Lord. Thank You for a safe and healthy birth of my baby at the appropriate time. Amen."*

The fear: I'll eat or drink the wrong thing and harm my baby

There are so many health alerts in the media these days and throughout all my pregnancies I have learnt about one more thing I am not supposed to eat whilst pregnant. Some I have eaten in previous pregnancies with no ill effects on my babies, so the key here is to be sensible. Listen to your health advisor, but don't panic if you eat something by mistake. Your parents didn't have any of these food alerts and you seemed to have turned out alright. Remember, God is in control of your pregnancy. The key is to trust Him.

"Dear Lord, thank You that You are in control of my pregnancy. Help me to show wisdom in my eating habits whilst pregnant. I pray that every food I eat and every medication I take will have no ill effects on my baby's health in the womb. I ask You to nourish and protect my baby [baby's prophetic name] as You knit them together in my womb. Lord, You have been so good to me by allowing this conception and Lord I trust You to bring my baby to me in fullness of health. You are a good God who gives good gifts. I thank You for the gift of this baby to me. Amen."

The fear: I'm stressed out. I'm worried, it's hurting the baby

Why is it that many of us in our first pregnancy decide to do two of the most stressful things in our lives? We either move home or start building works in our house! In all our eagerness to get things right for the new addition to the family we strive to decorate, buy the right things, and as we are getting steadily more tired with work, our home life and pregnancy, sometimes things get on top of us. While some studies show that acute, severe stress can increase a baby's risk for things like premature birth, experts agree that it's all about how you handle the situation. In other words, be practical in those times: go to bed earlier, rest, seek God, pray with your partner, pop on a worship song and rest in God's presence. God is the giver of peace in these times of craziness. Run to Him.

"Dear Lord, thank You that You say in John 14:27 that, 'I am leaving you with a gift—peace of mind and heart. And the peace I give is a gift the world cannot give. So don't be troubled or afraid.' Lord, reading Your Word brings comfort to me and I give all my stresses to You. Help me to be able to relax in Your presence and run into Your arms on those days when stress seems to grip me, so that I will turn to You Lord for that peace of mind and heart that only You can give. Give me peace with You during the day and deep sleep at nighttime. Help everything that needs to happen, happen with such ease. Let the busyness in my head calm and let me trust You that everything will work out with Your hand guiding my steps. God, I put my trust in You. Help me to feel Your peace. Let Your presence fill my womb right now. May no ill effect be passed on to my child, but surround them with Your love. I love You. Amen."

The fear: my baby will have a birth defect

This is a natural fear that almost every woman goes through at some point in her pregnancy. You want your child to be perfect and that is a perfectly normal desire. In fact, over 95% of babies are born without any defect, and the main advice out there is to make sure that you take your folic acid and prenatal vitamins, which help to keep you and your baby healthy. Always talk to your midwife or health practitioner about any concerns and they will be able to talk them through with you. Again, God is the centre of your pregnancy. He knew your child even before conception and has been carefully knitting them together in the womb. He is a creative God and knows the perfect baby for you.

> *"Dear Lord, I thank You that You say in Your Word that You have formed my baby's inward parts and knitted them together in my womb; that You have fearfully and wonderfully made my child (Psalm 139:13–16). I pray that You continue to help baby [baby's prophetic name] to develop correctly. I pray that baby [baby's prophetic name] is born with no abnormalities and that You will bring to us our beautiful baby at Your appointed time. I trust You God with my baby. Amen."*

The fear: I'll go into labour too early, or not be in my chosen place of birth

After my first born son (who was born in 4 hours 20mins, a little quick for a first time birth), I felt a little nervous before each labour, just in case we didn't get to the hospital in time. I had to trust that God really was in charge of all the details. He knew what I would be doing at the time I went into labour and how long the labour would be. Although you hear of some stories of women who don't quite make it to the labour room, first time pregnancy labours can be as long as 24 hours or more. God has your labour and the birth of your child in His perfect control. God knows when and where your baby will be born and the reasons for it, but most of the time you will make it to the hospital and you will know when you are in labour. If you are not sure, then you are probably not in labour. God has His perfect timing. Try to trust Him that He knows best for your unborn child and you.

"Dear Lord, I thank You that You love me and baby [baby's prophetic name]. I thank You that You have baby [baby's prophetic name]'s life all planned out for them. You are the Creator God and You are a God of order. When You made the heavens and the earth You created them at certain times and spoke life to see Your word become reality. You have already chosen Your time for my baby [baby's prophetic name] to come to this earth. I thank You that You will give me time to safely arrive at the birthing place of my child to deliver baby [baby's prophetic name] safely. You say in Your word that we should commit everything we do to You, Lord, and trust You and You will help us. You tell me to be still in Your presence Lord and wait patiently for You to act (Psalm 37:5–7). Help me to have that patience and trust in You as I commit this labour into Your hands. Amen."

The fear: I'll have complications like pre-eclampsia or gestational diabetes

Every person is different and every pregnancy is different. During each of my pregnancies different things have happened to my body. With my first pregnancy, towards the end, my ankles and feet were swollen and I couldn't fit my wedding ring on my finger due to my swollen hands. With my last pregnancy I was told I had gestational diabetes. All these added to the experience of pregnancy. I decided not to concentrate on the negatives that I could see, or was being told, but trusted God. I took and accepted the good advice from the medical professionals, but I also put my faith muscle into gear, trusting that God was and is the maker of me and my child.

Generally, the risk of developing dangerously high blood pressure (pre-eclampsia) is just between 5 and 8 percent. It's more common in women under 18 or over age 35, as well as in women who have borderline high blood pressure going into their pregnancy. But if you have any of these issues, your doctors will be monitoring you closely and will spot these conditions early. Remember, God has His hand on you and your child, as He is knitting away, bringing a child into your life that is best for you and His kingdom.

Through prayer we have seen these conditions reversed and good health preserved. We have also seen medical staff take wise decisions and God carry women on a journey of trust in Him. In all things, God is still in control.

"Dear Lord, thank You that You say in Your Word that: 'Blessed is the fruit of your body' (Deuteronomy 28:4) and where You have blessed, Your blessing stays. I claim that blessing upon my body and the body of my baby [baby's prophetic name] as You knit them together within my womb. I pause to consider the wondrous works of You my God (Job 37:14) and I dwell in the shelter of the Most High and I rest in the shadow of the Almighty. I will say of the Lord, You

are my refuge and my fortress, my God in whom I trust (Psalm 91:1). Your Word says in Isaiah 53:5 that Jesus took all my sickness and diseases and He carried my sorrows, so I receive healing now, as Jesus is my healer. I pray that my health will be good and strong throughout my pregnancy, and cast all my cares on You my Lord. Amen."

The fear: Labour will be too tough or painful, I'll never make it through

I have heard that labour can be described like your body flexing your muscles within your stomach. After 5 labours I would suggest that it is a little bit more intense than that, but depending on your pain threshold it is like having extremely strong period pains. The best way to deal with the fear of what labour will bring is to NOT listen to any people's stories about their labour and avoid hospital dramas that show dramatic scenes of childbirth. All these will feed your fear.

God broke the curse over our lives when He sent Jesus to die for our sins, and the revelation that Jesus is very present in the labour room, hand in hand with you, will help. Midwives can give you all the pain relief you need, if that is what you require, but God made it so that your body would cope with labour. Personally, I have always found that labour is the most enjoyable and exciting part of my pregnancy, as I will soon be meeting my little baby. Go in ready to enjoy it, switch your mind onto the positives and you will go in more relaxed and ready to cope.

"Dear Lord, as I come close to the birth of baby[baby's prophetic name], I feel a little apprehensive and I am struggling with a fear of the unknown, of what childbirth brings. Lord, You have taken care of me throughout my pregnancy and now that I come to the time of childbirth I need to know You will be with me through the labour. Let me feel the peace of Your presence so that when my contractions start, and in the midst of the intensity of labour, You will remain my focus. I trust You to give me the wisdom to ask for what I need, to listen to those who know better and to trust that Your hand is upon the birth of my baby. Thank You, Lord. Amen."

The following prayer is for those who may have had a less positive experience of labour in the past.

"Lord, You know my previous experience of labour and how it has put a shadow over this pregnancy.

Yet You do not want me to be bound by fear, so I ask You Lord to wipe from my mind my previous experiences of labour. I declare over this labour that it will be different to the one that went before. I ask You, Lord, to make this experience different from my previous one. Go into the labour room with me and give me Your peace as baby [baby's prophetic name] is born. I trust You to do something different this time. In Jesus' name. Amen."

The fear: I'm not going to be a good mum or dad

Steve Chalke says, "Before I got married I had around five theories on raising children and no children. Now I have five children and no theories."

I feel exactly the same way. My guess is that if you are reading this book to ensure that you are giving your child the very best you can before they are born, then you have started the journey of being a great mum, dad, role model and disciple maker of your children. The love for your child will grow with each day and your protection instincts will kick in. Every concern you have for their future shows your desire to send them in the right direction. Yes, you will make mistakes (I know we have), but being a parent is a constant learning experience to be enjoyed. God has allowed you to be a parent for a reason. There will be different seasons in your life as a parent, but determine to find God's best, no matter what each season brings to you.

> "Dear Lord, help me to be a good parent. Help me to be able to nurture and care for all the needs of my child. Help me to listen and respond with love and care and gentleness. Give me wisdom when they require discipline. Help me to have patience when I am tired. Show me how to train them in the way they should go, so that when they grow old they won't depart from it. Enable me to use my words to build them up and not to tear them down. Help me to bless them in their life, so that they will grow to be like oaks of righteousness displaying your splendour. Give me the wisdom I need to make the right decisions for their lives and help me to introduce them to You, Jesus, for their walk with you. Let my character show You to them. Where my parents set me a good example in child rearing, help me to copy them. Where I feel my parents failed me, help me not to repeat their mistakes with my own children. Continue to work in me to make me more like You. In Jesus' name. Amen."

The fear: other fears not covered above

Each of us will have to face different things in our lives. The prayer below is a general prayer to cover all fears.

> *"Dear Lord, thank You that You are God. I know that fear does not come from You. You have not put in me a spirit of fear, but of love, power and of a sound mind (2 Timothy 1:7). With this knowledge I reject all fear and ask You to come and fill me with the boldness of Your Holy Spirit. Forgive me when I have not trusted You and help me now to trust that You are in charge no matter what happens. I release all my fears to You and ask You to fill me with Your love now. In Jesus' name. Amen."*

Part 5

Appendices

A

A Word on Infertility

Many women's ideal dream is that one day they will meet their Prince Charming and then get married, followed by having a brood of near-perfect children to finish off their dream. But this is not necessarily how life pans out. The heartbreak and stress of infertility for any couple can sometimes place considerable strain on even the strongest marriage. For others, their journey is one of honouring God with their lives, longing for a family, but not even finding the Prince Charming to help their dreams come true.

When you cannot conceive there are feelings of hurt. There is the self-imposed perception of inadequacy. There is the repeated dashing of hopes, as you try every method under the sun, from monthly timings to taking your temperature each day in the hope of finding the perfect time, to medical interventions. Then there is the question: "Why me Lord? I would make such a great parent." All this is beyond what most women who have never had this issue could even try to comprehend.

If you are reading this as a couple who are struggling with infertility, it is possible you have already tied yourself up emotional knots, searching for reasons or points of blame. It is easy to feel very vulnerable and to allow fear and anxiety to take hold. As a Christian, your mind can take you to the strangest places about why God is letting this happen. It takes a lot of courage to focus on a loving God who is capable of all things, and has a bigger picture of our lives than we will ever have. We don't always have a reason why, even though it is the first question we want God to answer.

Yet the Bible is not silent on this issue. A number of women struggled with infertility in the Bible. These women had been crying out to God for some time before He answered. They knew the pain of infertility. Every person has a different burden to bear in life and infertility can be one of the hardest of them all.

These women in the Bible had seen their friends having children without difficulty. They had listened to their friends complaining about sleepless nights and tantrums and knew that such "trials" were nothing compared to having no children. They had to face down friends and relatives who were asking, "So, are you planning to have children soon?"

In some cases, like Sarah, it is clear that they gave up all hope of ever having a child. For others, like Rachel, it put a great strain on the relationship between husband and wife.

In every case they went on to give birth to some of the most significant people in Bible history. Perhaps the waiting and longing led to a deeper consecration of their children when they finally came. In the case of Hannah, we know that she made a deep vow to God that she fulfilled when God finally blessed her with a child.

Take a look at each of these infertile parents who gave birth to a God-ordained child:

- Abraham and Sarah gave birth to Isaac (Genesis 11:30)
- Isaac and Rebekah gave birth to Jacob and Esau (Genesis 25:21)
- Jacob and Rachel gave birth to Joseph (Genesis 30:1)
- Manoah and his wife gave birth to Samson (Judges 13:2)
- Elkanah and Hannah gave birth to Samuel (1 Samuel 1:5)
- Zechariah and Elizabeth gave birth to John the Baptist (Luke 1:7)

The Bible also shows us that it is God who gives us children.

> *"When the Lord saw that Leah was unloved, He enabled her to have children, but Rachel could not conceive."*
>
> Genesis 29:31

> *"Then Jacob became furious with Rachel. 'Am I God?' he asked. 'He's the one who has kept you from having children!'"*
>
> Genesis 30:2

Some people have been blessed with one child, but then suffer from secondary infertility and are unable to get pregnant again. I have a friend who has struggled with secondary infertility. She is the most amazing mum to her incredible son, but has since had several miscarriages. She is a natural mother, but that longing is very real. It doesn't negate the wonderful son she already has, but her desire for another child is so strong that she is willing to suffer the trauma of repeated miscarriages on the off chance that one child may survive. These feelings of grief are very real for every woman who desires a child and God is very aware of this.

Armed with this Bible knowledge, how can it help us to cope with infertility?

Firstly, we can admit the feelings. God has heard it all before and understands the different emotions, from pain to isolation, from doubt to despair. Pour your heart out to God. Just like Hannah wept before God, do not be afraid to weep before Him. The writer in Proverbs understood the continual nature of the grief that comes with infertility.

> *"There are three things that are never satisfied, Four*
> *never say, 'Enough!': The grave, The barren womb,*
> *The earth that is not satisfied with water—And the*
> *fire never says, 'Enough!'"*
>
> Proverbs 30:15–16

Secondly, wait on God. God is the one who gives us children. He is the one who knows the plan for your life. He knows whether your infertility will be for a season or for life. As you spend time with God, ask for His clarity and direction in this matter. Take time as husband and wife to pray and wait on God together. For some, God will lead you to various types of infertility treatment. For others, God will give you an assurance that your time will come. For others, He will give you faith to believe Him for something that the doctors have said is impossible. For others, God will give you peace with your situation.

Finally, make the most of your life. Determine to make the most of the life God has given you. Most women have very maternal instincts, so this is easier said than done. Yet you are not defined by your fertility as a couple, you are defined by your standing before God. See how you can take what He has given you and use it for good. Many ministries draw on the maternal urges and gifts that God has placed in you. Allow God to lead you into your destiny where you can be fulfilled. Some may choose formally to adopt a child, while others will look for people of all ages who are in need of a family and be that family for them.

> *"'Sing, O childless woman, you who have never given birth! Break into loud and joyful song, O Jerusalem, you who have never been in labour. For the desolate woman now has more children than the woman who lives with her husband,' says the Lord. 'Enlarge your house; build an addition. Spread out your home, and spare no expense! For you will soon be bursting at the seams. Your descendants will occupy other nations and resettle the ruined cities.'"*
>
> Isaiah 54:1–3

In all of this, ask God to help you to trust Him. You may not understand why you are having to face this pain, but God's plan for you is good.

> *"'For I know the plans I have for you,' says the Lord. 'They are plans for good and not for disaster, to give you a future and a hope. In those days when you pray, I will listen. If you look for me wholeheartedly, you will find Me.'"*
>
> Jeremiah 29:11–13

One couple's journey

The husband writes: "Wheng and I have been married since 2006. After a while we began to try for a baby, but nothing was working. So many people gave us advice about what we should try, but nothing was effective. After a few years of trying for a baby we took the decision to go to the doctors to see how they could help.

"After they had heard our story they sent us for lots of different tests at the hospital. When the results came back they were devastating. My sperm count was too low and my wife's hormone count was too high. The doctors told us there was no chance of us having a baby and that there were no other options they could offer us. By now I was 40 years old and Wheng was 41.

"During all this time we thought Wheng was pregnant, only to find out that it was a false alarm. This happened over and over again. These occasions were so hard for my wife to go through and it was hard for me to see her so upset.

"In our church I had been teaching the children for twenty years. Now some of the children I had taught had become parents themselves. We saw young couples marry after us, who then became parents. It was so hard for us to see and to hear other people's good news.

"I believe the one thing that gave us our patient reward was that we kept out hearts right and rejoiced with those who became pregnant before us. We also made a decision that we would not allow this to stop us from teaching other people's children, but instead we would teach them as if they were ours.

"Lastly, we have a great church and pastors who prayed, encouraged and stayed in faith with us. I believe the Lord saw our hearts and rewarded our faith and patience through this challenging time.

"Without any medical intervention our son Samuel was born on 5 December 2014. After eight long years of waiting God had made the impossible possible for us."

The wife writes: "To begin with it was very hard, but then I decided to give up trying and give the situation to the Lord. I determined to live and enjoy my married life to the full and to stop stressing over having a child. I chose to trust the Lord, whatever His plan was for us, giving thanks to Him no matter what was the outcome."

Our hearts go out to those women who have a strong desire for a child of their own, but for some reason this is not happening. We wish we had all the answers to the questions that plague these women's minds, but we don't. We cannot really try to understand, but we can recommend an appropriate book called *Babies Don't Grow On Trees, At Least Not in My Garden* by Talitha Ishi-Smith. It is a long overdue, frank, honest and liberating read for anyone who has been impacted by infertility. Talitha is a lady who has struggled but come to terms with this journey in her life and has expressed herself with such a powerful beauty that it may be of help to other ladies in a similar situation.

May this trial draw you nearer to God and may He give you the desires of your heart.

For Personal Reflection

Admit your feelings

Wait on God

Make the most of your life

A prayer for a woman:

> *"Lord, you know my pain. You know my fears. You know my longing and my heart's desire. I simply ask you grant me a child. May any child you give me be devoted to service in your kingdom for your glory. God, the Giver of life, I ask you for a child. In Jesus' Name. Amen."*

A prayer for couples:

> *"Lord, you know our pain. You know our fears. You know our longing and our heart's desire. Strengthen our relationship with each other and with you during this testing time as we choose to trust you in spite of our pain. We simply ask you grant us a child. May any child you give us be devoted to service in your kingdom for your glory. God, the Giver of life, we ask you for a healthy child. In Jesus' Name. Amen."*

B

Setting up a Womb Ministry

A church has many meetings and ministries to reach people, from birth to the elderly, but one age that is often forgotten is the unborn child. As we seen in this book, children in the womb are responsive to God's Spirit. For many women there is a strong spiritual element to pregnancy as they consider new life.

One great way to reach out to pregnant women in your community/church is to set up a womb ministry to support them and their partners through pregnancy. This can provide a forum in which you can share some of the principles in this book with a wider number of people in your church, as well as providing support at a critical point of their lives.

We have found ministry to the womb often takes on a very prophetic edge as God reveals His plans for children and reassures parents for the future. This section will provide a model of some of the things that we have done. We encourage you to consider doing something similar.

Hold a monthly meeting

We invited mums and dads to join together at the meeting. Each month we would include the following elements:

- Fresh fruit, snacks and drinks ready to welcome people. As well as being a great way to make people feel welcome, it can help keep hunger at bay—something many pregnant women will be very grateful for

- Time for parents and the team to mix, share together and get to know each other

- Speak out declarations together as a group. There is power in our words and as we join in faith together for our families it can be a great source of encouragement to all

- Pray and prophesy over the families

- Teaching times. Many of these sessions can be run on a rolling programme so that over the 7–9 months of attendance most parents will get to be part of most sessions. For some sessions we would separate the mums from the dads at the teaching time and run sessions applicable for their different roles.

A great starting point for topics could be the different chapters in this book. In addition to this teaching, here are some other suggestions of topics you could cover:

- Pregnancy from a Christian midwife's perspective.

- Pamper those ladies—get a beautician in who is willing to give some free time to the church for pregnant ladies. Find a masseur who can teach dads how to deliver that soothing massage.

- Tips for dad from other dads.

- Feed that baby and you—nutritional advice.

- Paediatrician's talk on baby development.

- Bring and take week—ask your church if there is anything people don't need and are willing to give to new mums and dads to be.

- Baby Shower/thanksgiving week. This session became an annual event for us as we invited all the families who had been in contact with the womb ministry to come and join us to give thanks to God for their babies.

- Practical and spiritual things you should know in preparing for labour.

- Parenting seminar—preparation for after your child is born.

- Testimony time—previous womb ministry members loved to come back and share their stories.

- All about the children's and family ministry in the church.

We also had a board on which we wrote the names of couples who were desiring children but were not able to conceive. There is something special about those who are pregnant praying for the blessing of children for those who cannot conceive. Many of the couples we prayed for joined the womb ministry the following year as God opened their wombs.

Support outside the meetings

Intercession prayer line. All the parents who came to the womb ministry were given a contact phone number that they could call whenever they needed prayer. Parents felt so supported to know that there was a team of people ready to pray for them.

We encouraged all parents to let us know when they went into labour so that we could pray. They also called when doctors gave bad news, when they were worried about anything or when issues in their family flared up. This was not a counselling line or a medical hotline, it was simply a prayer line.

A team of intercessors with a heart for babies and families were committed to praying as text messages and emails were sent to them.

Starter pack. As each parent-to-be joins you, why not prepare a welcome pack for the womb ministry. It could include:

- birth declaration
- a copy of this book (or another book on the spirituality of children in the womb)
- a pregnancy CD for expectant mums for them to relax in God's presence
- an introduction to the womb ministry—who's who and what to expect
- dates of the next six months of meetings
- details of the intercession hotline

Congratulations. Once a baby has been born, be ready to send out a card of congratulations. Some churches arrange a meal rota so that different members of the congregation deliver food to the house for the first couple of weeks after the baby is born. This practical help can be a real support as new parents adjust to having a baby.

Send an information pack on recommended Bible books and music for babies and young children as well as details of what is available in your church for babies and toddlers.

Get people involved

The success of such a ministry is dependent on the people who are part of the team. We recommend having strong intercessors and people who move in the prophetic on the team, as well as someone from the medical profession (such as a midwife).

Take a look at the skill sets of the people in your congregation: midwives, beauticians, pastors, paediatricians and parents all have something that could enrich your sessions.

Get in touch with a maternity shop and ask for any clothing that is out of season or not saleable to give away to the ladies for free as a tax deductible charity donation.

Gather a group of intercessors in your church who are prepared to pray for the ladies and their partners by name throughout their pregnancy and labour. They don't need to attend the meetings, but will be steadfast in their prayers for the unborn children and their parents. I gathered a lot of faith throughout my pregnancies thanks to our intercessory team who prayed for me through difficult seasons and through the labour process. There truly is power in the prayers of these amazing people. Set up an intercession board for all the ladies who would like prayer throughout their pregnancy, so anybody who has a heart will pray for them.

Nana's testimony—a midwife in womb ministry

"The monthly meetings are a blessing and a joyous occasion as we share thoughts, feelings, ideas and experiences about pregnancy, childbirth and also pray together for our unborn babies and families. We've seen husbands and wives unite, men begin to recognise themselves as heads of the household and begin to take their God-given authority as the head and spiritual leader of the family.

"As one of the midwives in the team, I have not only seen miracles happen to childbearing women and their families, but the hand of God has moved on my family too and is still moving. I recommend the womb ministry to anybody who can make any contribution whatsoever to families. Come and be a part of the team and your life will never be the same."

C

It's OK to Laugh

Questions and answers

Q. Should I have a baby after 35?
A. No, 35 children is enough

Q. I'm 2 months pregnant now, when will my baby move?
A. Probably right after they finish college.

Q. What is the most reliable method to determine a baby's sex?
A. Childbirth

Q. Do I have to have a baby shower?
A. Not if you change the baby's nappy very quickly

Q. Since I became pregnant, my breasts, rear end, and even my feet have grown. Is there anything that gets smaller during pregnancy?
A. Yes, your bladder.

Q. Where is the best place to store breast milk?
A. In your breasts.

The difference between siblings

Your clothes
1st baby: You begin wearing maternity clothes as soon as the pregnancy test comes back positive.
2nd baby: You wear your regular clothes for as long as possible.
3rd baby: Your maternity clothes are your regular clothes.

Preparing for the birth
1st baby: You practice your breathing religiously.
2nd baby: You don't bother because you remember that last time, breathing didn't do a thing.
3rd baby: You ask for an epidural in your eighth month.

Baby's clothes

1st baby: You pre-wash your newborn's clothes, colour coordinate them and fold them neatly in the baby's little bureau.

2nd baby: You check to make sure that the clothes are clean and discard only the ones with the darkest stains.

3rd baby: Boys can wear pink, can't they?

Worries

1st baby: At the first sign of distress—a whimper, a frown—you pick up the baby.

2nd baby: You pick the baby up when her wails threaten to wake your firstborn.

3rd baby: You teach your three-year-old how to rewind the mechanical swing.

Dummy/pacifier

1st baby: If the dummy falls on the floor, you put it away until you can go home and wash and boil it.

2nd baby: When the dummy falls on the floor, you squirt it off with some juice from the baby's bottle.

3rd baby: You wipe it off on your shirt and pop it back in.

Nappies/diapers

1st baby: You change your baby's nappies every hour, whether they need it or not.

2nd baby: You change their nappy every two to three hours, if needed.

3rd baby: You try to change their nappy before others start to complain about the smell or you see it sagging to their knees.

Activities

1st baby: You take your infant to Baby Gymnastics, Baby Swing, and Baby Story Hour.

2nd baby: You take your infant to Baby Gymnastics.

3rd baby: You take your infant to the supermarket and the dry cleaners.

Going out

1st baby: The first time you leave your baby with a sitter, you call home five times.

2nd baby: Just before you walk out the door, you remember to leave a number where you can be reached.

3rd baby: You leave instructions for the sitter to call only if she sees blood.

At home

1st baby: You spend a good bit of every day just gazing at the baby.

2nd baby: You spend a bit of everyday watching to be sure your older child isn't squeezing, poking, or hitting the baby.

3rd baby: You spend a little bit of every day hiding from the children.

Swallowing coins

1st child: When first child swallows a coin, you rush the child to the hospital and demand x-rays.

2nd child: When second child swallows a coin, you carefully watch for the coin to pass.

3rd child: When third child swallows a coin you deduct it from his allowance.

D

Recommended Resources

Related resources from Children Can

Jesus, Your Baby and You, Prayer Journal by Helen and Olly Goldenberg

The Josiah Generation by Olly Goldenberg—an inspirational book that sets out the call on this generation and shows how God is using children in this world.

At Home with God by Olly Goldenberg—this book looks at how we can pass on our faith to our children.

Jesus, Your Baby and You soaking CD for pregnant women. Sit back, relax and enjoy God's presence.

I love Jesus CD by Olly Goldenberg (Children Can)—music for newborns, not-yet-borns and toddlers. Great to sing to your baby in pregnancy. They will come out knowing the tunes and ready to praise.

Birthing Declaration Prayer Card. A handy card with the prayer declarations from part 4, for you to put on your wall or carry around with you.

Things to Do

Do this once:

- Prayerfully choose a prophetic name for your child (and use it regularly)
- Hold a prayer shower

Do this regularly:

- Say the birth declaration and use the prayer scriptures for your baby
- Pray as a family for the baby
- Write in your pregnancy prayer journal
- Take time to worship God and soak in His presence

Authors' Note on Healing

We believe that God can and does cure people miraculously today. However, we do not believe that this is the only way that God will work. God gives wisdom and knowledge to us to help us fight medical problems. Medical care can be part of God's plan for bringing relief and healing to His people. However, medicine still does not hold all the answers. We are in favor of both competent medical treatment and the power of prayer. We would not encourage anyone to neglect either of these during their time of need. This book is not intended to be a source of medical advice, but rather of spiritual instruction and support.

Authors' Contact Information

Olly & Helen Goldenberg

BM Children Can, London, WC1N 3XX, UK.

info@childrencan.co.uk

www.childrencan.co.uk